I0025212

Henry de Rosenbach Walker

Australasian Democracy

Henry de Rosenbach Walker

Australasian Democracy

ISBN/EAN: 9783744752664

Printed in Europe, USA, Canada, Australia, Japan

Cover: Foto ©ninafisch / pixelio.de

More available books at **www.hansebooks.com**

AUSTRALASIAN

DEMOCRACY

BY

HENRY DE R. WALKER

LONDON

T. FISHER UNWIN

PATERNOSTER SQUARE

MDCCCXCVII

PREFACE

THE following pages have been written from the point of view of the year 1896, the greater part of which I spent in Australia. During the earlier months of the present year I was in New Zealand, but I was unable to continue my survey of general Australasian affairs.

A result of the limitation that I was compelled to impose upon myself will be observed in the apparent antiquity of the chapter dealing with Australian Federation ; but this is not so great as might have been anticipated, the new Federal Convention having drafted a Bill which is based, to a large extent, upon that of 1891. For purposes of comparison I have, with the kind permission of the London agents of the Melbourne *Argus*, included an article in which that newspaper has summarised the provisions of the new Federal Constitution Bill.

I have also included a brief account of a visit to the Coolgardie goldfields which, though alien in purpose from the remaining chapters, may not be without interest as a record of personal impressions of a Province which has but recently felt the effects of a budding prosperity.

It has been suggested to me that I should attempt to discuss Australasian problems with reference to their applicability to Great Britain ; but I have preferred to leave this task, of which the importance cannot be overstated, to persons of greater experience, and to confine myself to a record of Australasian action and to a comparison of the points of similarity or the reverse between the several Provinces. It will be seen, however, that, in some cases, as when dealing, for instance, with the results of payment of members and with the powers and privileges of Australasian Upper Houses, I have noted differences of conditions which must render deductions by analogy a matter of extreme difficulty.

The terms " Liberal" and " Conservative" are used to denote, respectively, the more and the less advanced parties in Australasian politics, and must not be taken to imply differences in opinion similar to those prevailing in Great Britain.

In conclusion, I would only say that my studies would have been impossible in the absence of kindly communicativeness on the part of politicians of all shades of opinion ; and, on the social side, that I retain warm feelings of gratitude towards the committees of clubs and numerous acquaintances who extended to me the cordial hospitality of kinship.

H. DE R. WALKER.

23, CORK STREET, W.,

July 25, 1897.

CONTENTS

I.

LIBERALISM AND LABOUR IN SOUTH AUSTRALIA.

II.

DEMOCRACY AND ITS SAFEGUARDS IN NEW SOUTH WALES.

LIBERALISM AND LABOUR IN SOUTH AUSTRALIA

Contrast between Western Australia and the Eastern Provinces—
The Constitution of South Australia—The alliance between
Liberalism and Labour—Joint action in the face of financial
depression : Village Settlements, Progressive Taxation, the
direct encouragement of production—The advocacy of an
Elective Executive—The State and Religious Instruction.

THE traveller who visited Western Australia in 1896 saw a country which was enjoying, owing to its goldfields, a phenomenally rapid development, with all its attendant advantages of a large increase in population, an expanding revenue, and abundance of employment. As he passed to the Eastern Provinces he found himself in the midst of communities which had been shaken to their foundations by the fall in the value of their staple products and the collapse of many banking institutions, and were putting forth strenuous efforts to restore the equilibrium between revenue and expenditure and to make a fresh start upon the path of prosperity. These efforts, varying in detail in different Provinces, have included the imposition

2

of additional taxation, provision for the unemployed, and, in some cases, direct encouragement of production. The policy pursued by South Australia is of particular interest as her Constitution gives the freest play to democratic influences.

The House of Assembly is elected on the basis of adult suffrage ; the Upper House or Legislative Council by adults possessing a property qualification consisting of a freehold of the clear annual value of £50, a registered leasehold of £20, with three years to run or the right of purchase, or the occupation of a dwelling-house of the clear annual value of £25. No property qualification is required in candidates for election to either House, and the Members of both Houses are paid at the rate of £200 per annum. Adults, upon reaching the age of twenty-one in the case of the Assembly or possessing the requisite qualification in the case of the Council, can claim to be placed upon the electoral roll and are entitled to vote upon the expiration of six months after registration ; upon removal to another constituency, the vote can immediately be transferred. Plural voting is forbidden under heavy penalties, and all the elections, except that for the Northern Territory, take place upon the same day.

These conditions have enabled the democratic element to obtain a preponderating voice in both Houses, by a majority of one in the Council and by a considerable majority in the Assembly. During

the last three years the Government has been in the
hands of the Liberals under the Hon. C. C. Kingston, who has included in his cabinet two former
Premiers in the persons of the Treasurer, the Hon.
F. W. Holder, and the Minister of Education and
Agriculture, the Hon. Dr. Cockburn. The Ministerialists have had the support of the Labour Party,
which has been very successful with its candidates
and now holds the balance of power. It was formed
towards the close of the year 1890, after the failure
of the maritime strike, in response to the feeling of
the Trades Unions and other labour organisations
that their objects would be obtained most easily by
securing the direct representation of labour in Parliament. They were influenced also by the rejection
by the Assembly of Dr. Cockburn's proposals for
progressive taxation in spite of promises made by a
majority of the members before their election. A
political programme was, accordingly, drawn up,
which is the accepted creed of the Labour representatives, who number six in the Council of
twenty-four and twelve in the Assembly of fifty-
four members. It has successively been modified, as
measures previously advocated have been passed
into law, and contains the following principal
items : The cessation of the alienation of Crown
Lands by the substitution of some system of leasing;
the remission of the duties on articles not grown or
produced in the Colony, any resulting deficiency in
the revenue to be made up by increasing the tax on

land values; redistribution of seats on the basis of population; the encouragement of local industries by the extension of the State Export Department, so that producers may be able to, obtain the full benefit of foreign markets; and Federation on a democratic basis. The Labour Party are opposed most strongly to the admission of coloured races and to assisted immigration, on the ground that the former would lower the status of the Australian workman, and the latter cause the supply of labour to exceed the demand and bring misery and destitution upon the poor. The relations of the Labour and Liberal members, which have been most cordial, are based upon mutual interdependence. The Liberals rely upon the support of the Labour members; the latter are not strong enough to take office, nor, I understand, do they wish to do so, and must support the Liberals in order to be able to mould the legislation to the shape that they desire. A prominent member of the Labour Party has thus summarised the position : "The hardest work in connection with some of the measures has been done by Liberals who, though not members of the Party, are generally found working in connection with that body. But it must be conceded that most of the planks which have been carried owe their early success to the fact of their adoption on the programme of the United Labour Party, and the persistent advocacy and solid votes of its members." The policy of the Party has created a great amount of bitterness in the country, their successful advocacy of progressive taxation on incomes and land values and of other democratic measures having led them to be charged with being inimical to capital as such ; but the Speaker of the Assembly, who is a Conservative, has stated in a recent speech that, "in speaking of the Labour Party, he wishes to do so with the greatest respect. They are a power in the House, and no Government could have retained office in the last Parliament without their support. The Labour representatives were picked men, clever in debate, unremitting in attention to their duties, and a credit to the districts they represented." The leader of the Party is Mr. J. A. McPherson, a native of Aberdeen, who migrated to Adelaide in 1882 and engaged in the printing trade. He identified himself with Trades Union affairs, was elected unanimously in 1890 to be Secretary of the Trades and Labour Council, and still holds that position. He entered the Assembly at a bye-election in 1892, and is regarded as one of the ablest and most energetic members of the Labour Party. Mr. McPherson has a popular supporter in Mr. E. L. Batchelor, the colleague of the Premier in the representation of West Adelaide, who has risen from subordinate employment on the Government railways to be, at the age of thirty, President of the Railway Association and Secretary of the Party. Mr. Batchelor is a man of broad views and a keen student, and has brought forward a Bill for the institution of the initiative and referendum, which he considers to be suited to the small population of South Australia. The Party are fortunate in their leading men and show no signs of cleavage, their only serious difference of opinion having been in regard to the qualifications of Labour candidates. As long as solidarity can be maintained and the present leaders remain in the ascendant, no fear need be felt that they will subordinate the interests of the community to those of their own class, though they would be the first to admit that their main object is to protect the working man and to improve his position.

The principal measures of the present Administration, such as the Taxation Acts and the establishment of the Village Settlements and of the Produce Export Department, may be said to be the joint product of the Liberal and Labour Parties, and may be regarded as an example of the policy pursued by a pure democracy in the face of financial depression, dislocation of trade, and widespread scarcity of employment.

The object of the Act of 1893 which authorised the formation of Village Settlements was to prevent men of small means, who found difficulty in obtaining employment, from leaving the country by affording them the opportunity of settling upon the land and working it co-operatively with the assistance of advances from the State. Its main provisions were, that any twenty or more persons might form an association for the purpose of taking up a grant of land not exceeding 160 acres per head ; that the work should be done under the direction of trustees appointed by members of the association from among their number, who should manage the affairs of the village upon principles of co-operation and equitable division ; and that the Commissioner of Crown Lands might advance to any such association out of funds provided by Parliament, an amount not exceeding the sum of £50 for each villager and not exceeding one-half the cost of the improvements upon the land. The advances were to be repaid in ten equal annual instalments, with interest computed at 5 per cent. per annum on the moneys for the time being remaining unpaid ; but the first of such instalments was not to be payable until after the expiration of three years from the date of the advance. The formation of settlements on a purely communistic basis was rendered possible by Section 78 of the Act, which states that "the rules" (of an association) "may require payment to a common fund or otherwise as may be determined of all or any part of the earnings of the villagers whether earned within the village or elsewhere." Twelve associations were formed, mostly on the banks of the Murray, between the months of February and August, 1894, but not, with a single exception, on the lines intended by the Government. The extreme scarcity of employment and great poverty at Adelaide and in the neighbourhood in the early part of that year led them to form the remainder of persons who were almost entirely destitute. They were necessarily assisted at the start, but did not afterwards receive advances until the Government Inspector had certified that they were justified by the improvements made upon the land. The action of the Government was illegal throughout, as the Act stated expressly that the advances should be made out of funds provided by Parliament, and no funds had been voted for the purpose, but it may be condoned on the ground of the extreme urgency of the crisis. At the expiration of a year the limit had been reached in most cases, and further advances were indispensable to prevent the immediate collapse of the majority of the settlements. The Commissioner of Crown Lands, accordingly, introduced a Bill in which he asked for authority to increase the advances, under the same conditions, to £100 per head, and for further powers of control over the settlements. The Bill, which was hotly opposed, was not passed till a Select Committee had been appointed to inquire on the spot into the conditions and financial prospects of the settlements and had reported in its favour.

The report, which was dated November 14, 1895, and the evidence upon which it was based, gave a complete picture of the disadvantages under which the settlers laboured and of the drawbacks of the system of distribution. The land selected for the villages was such, it was pointed out, that it could not be cultivated except under irrigation. This had necessitated the erection of a costly pumping plant, which the settlers had difficulty in purchasing, as they could offer no security for payment. When the plant was finally obtained, it was found, in some cases, to be unsuitable ; in others it could not be properly worked in the absence of a capable engineer. The settlers, brought together at haphazard by destitution and not by their knowledge of agricultural pursuits, had wasted much time and labour through ignorance, incapacity, and insufficiency of proper tools. They had lacked a strong controlling hand to direct their operations, and had disobeyed the trustees whom they had themselves appointed ; and as the trustees had little power discipline had been nonexistent, and quarrels, at several settlements, of continual occurrence. Order had been restored with difficulty, as the only punishment was expulsion, upon a decision of the trustees ratified by a vote of the villagers, and many villagers had voted against expulsion from the fear that they in their turn might be subjected to a similar penalty. The arrangements for the distribution of rations also had caused considerable dissatisfaction and led to disagreement between single and married men, as the former felt that the latter received a share of the stores out of proportion to the work they had done. The general system was, that rations were issued on a sliding scale, according as a man was single or had a large or small family, and was to that extent purely communistic.

The difficulties encountered by the settlers had been such as would have discouraged most men, but, in spite of them, the total number had only fallen in eighteen months from 598 to 440, and the majority of witnesses expressed themselves satisfied with their lot. They admitted the necessity of further advances, but pleaded that they had a heavy burden to bear in the cost of machinery, and that their labour, especially in the planting of fruit trees, could not yield an immediate return. The financial position was thus summarised : — The Government had advanced £26,000, the unpaid accounts amounted to about £11,000, and the improvements were valued by the Commissioner of Crown Lands at £41,000.

During 1896 the further advances had been expended, but the settlements had not become self-supporting, and the increased burden of debt and uncertainty as to the future had caused many of the settlers to become disheartened and others to leave in despair. On the other hand, the appointment of an expert to exercise the additional powers conferred upon the Commissioner and to give advice to the settlers, had led to the diminution of quarrels and disagreements among them and to a better direction of their work. In view of these facts the Government decided to close four of the settlements which had been formed upon land unsuitable to the purpose, owing to the poorness of the soil or the absence of facilities for profitable irrigation. It has been

estimated that the remainder have sufficient irrigable
land to maintain a population of about three hundred
families, and that they require an average of about
£25 per settler to make them self-supporting. A
few enthusiasts alone believe that any portion of the
principal of the loans will ever be repaid; but the
Government will have no cause to complain if they
receive regular interest on the money. Some
difficulty is likely to arise in the disposal of the
produce. There is a considerable market for vege-
tables on the river, but it will soon be overtaken by
the supply. The settlers will probably devote most
of their land to fruit growing and dairying, and will
be able to take advantage of the Export Department.

The settlers should have a better chance of success in the future, as loafers are gradually being
weeded out, and the process is to be continued
until the settlers shall have been reduced to such as
have shown an honest desire to make homes for
themselves and their families upon the land. This
course has been rendered possible by the large exodus
of working men to Western Australia, which has
reduced the pressure upon the local labour market.
The Government desire to approximate all the
settlements to the level of Murtho, which alone was
formed of persons who had considerable means of
their own. The settlers, about twenty in number,
put an average of £60 each into the venture and left
good situations out of enthusiasm for the principles
of co-operation. They are intelligent, well-educated

men and women who are bound to put forward every effort to be successful, as otherwise they will be in a worse position than at the start. They work all the land upon the method of joint cultivation on the ground that, as different forms of produce are grown, it is of importance to be able to concentrate the greater portion of the labour at any point where it may be required, and, under the influence of communistic ideas, give to all an equal share of the results of their united efforts. This system would have seemed, from the constitution of human nature, to be doomed to failure ; but an amount of work has been done in planting and clearing which testifies to continuous and sustained labour, disagreements have been rare, and the settlers, in conversation with me, expressed themselves as contented with their lot and confident of eventual success. They do not regard themselves as recipients of charity, as they have received advances on the same conditions as holders of Working Men's blocks ; on the contrary, they regard themselves as pioneers of a new movement, and desire, not only to make homes for themselves and their families, but to prove that land can be worked successfully on a co-operative, almost a communistic, basis. If the Murtho settlers succeed, they will do so by the continued exercise of mutual forbearance and from the impulse of a common enthusiasm.

The Government appear to have made several

grave mistakes of omission and commission in the
formation of the settlements. They should have
caused a survey of the Murray lands to be made
before the selection of the sites, and they should
have realised that men, united only by their destitution, required control and direction, and, as the
majority were ignorant of agricultural pursuits,
constant superintendence of their work. The
system of joint cultivation also was entirely un-
suited to the class of men who formed the bulk
of the settlers. It is true that the Act authorised
neither preliminary surveys nor the appointment
of superintendents, and stated expressly that the
associations were to be co-operative; but if the
urgency of the crisis may be taken to have justified
the Government in making advances without the
sanction of Parliament, it would also have justified
such further illegalities as would have benefited the
settlers and safeguarded the interests of the taxpayers.

A certain amount of co-operation was inevitable
if the settlements were to be formed upon land
which could only be cultivated under irrigation, in
the erection of the pumping plant and the use of
water. It would also be advisable in the purchase
of seeds, trees and vines, the disposal of produce
and the common ownership of horses and implements of husbandry. But the land might have
been cut up into blocks, in order to enable each
settler to obtain the full benefit of his exertions

subject to payment for the services rendered to him by the association.

The Government are to be congratulated, however faulty their methods may have been, upon their attempt to enable the unemployed to make homes for themselves upon the land, a great improvement upon the policy of their predecessors, who wasted thousands of pounds upon unnecessary relief works. They have undoubtedly raised the moral tone of the settlers, who make a good impression upon the visitor through their intelligence and sobriety and the happy appearance of their children, and one cannot but regret that, owing to the absence of direction, much of their labour has been absolutely valueless. The cynic will say that the men have every reason to be contented as they are living entirely upon advances and can rid themselves of all responsibility for the loans by leaving the settlements; but he forgets that they have qualified for these advances by hard work and that they never see a shilling that they can call their own.

The whole question must be looked at from the point of view of the Australian, who would be horrified at our system, under which indigence is assumed to be the result of idleness and improvidence and relief is offered under the most degrading conditions, and expects his Government to do something to relieve the misery caused by scarcity of employment. In South Australia, where adult suffrage and payment of the members of both

Houses have made the working classes masters of
the situation, they can compel the Ministry to pay
attention to their wishes. A step in the right
direction was taken when Village Settlements were
substituted for temporary relief works; but any
future scheme, while affording to men the opportunity of regaining a position of independence,
should compel them to prove their worthiness by
their own individual exertions.

The wide application by the Australasian Provinces of the principle of State action renders them
especially liable to violent fluctuations of prosperity
and adversity. As young countries they have
borrowed largely for purposes of development,
and have constructed expensive public works which
have greatly increased the demand for labour.
During the recent years of depression the Government have been obliged to discontinue their operations, and have offered less employment at a time
when the labour market was already overstocked
owing to the contraction of private enterprise.
Similarly in the case of revenue : the receipts from
the railways, which are almost universally owned by
the State, vary proportionately with the returns from
taxation, which depend in their turn largely upon
the condition of trade. They have fallen in South
Australia from £1,229,598 in 1891–2 to £967,656
in 1894–5, with the result that when the community
has been least able, owing to the diminished returns
from other resources of revenue, to bear additional

taxation, further taxes have necessarily been imposed to meet the interest upon the loans out of the proceeds of which the railways have been constructed. The Kingston Government, which took office in 1893, had to face a deficit of £200,000, and immediately set to work to restore order in the finances. This they attempted to do by retrenchment, reducing the expenditure by £100,000 per annum, and by the imposition of fresh taxation. Succession Duties, a tax on the unimproved value of land and an income tax had already been imposed, a distinction being made in the latter case, between incomes derived from property and incomes resulting from personal exertion ; but the present Government were the first to introduce the progressive principle into the taxes on incomes and land values. This legislation has encountered, as might be expected, the strongest opposition from the richer members of the community, who protest that a feeling of insecurity is produced and capital driven out of the country, but it may be noted that South Australia in 1895 raised money at 3 per cent. upon exceptionally favourable terms. The Government were compelled to obtain further funds, and showed their desire to equalise the incidence of the additional taxes by lowering, in spite of the opposition of the Labour Party, the exemption from income tax from £200 to £125 and by increasing the duty on beer, spirits, and other articles of ordinary consumption. Income tax is

at present at the rate of 4½d. in the pound up to
£800, and of 6d. in the pound above £800 of taxable
amount resulting from personal exertions, and at
the rate of 9d. and 1s. in the pound, respectively,
on incomes from property. Incomes between £125
and £425 enjoy exemption on £125 of the amount.
Taxpayers are required, under penalty of prosecution for perjury for a false declaration, to furnish
annually a statement of all forms of income that
they have enjoyed during the past year, except in
respect of any share or interest in a registered
company ; in this case the tax, at the rate of a
shilling in the pound, is deducted by an officer
of the company before payment of the dividends
to shareholders. The higher rate is not paid on
either form of income unless it, separately, exceeds
£800. The tax on the unimproved value of land
is ½d. in the pound up to, and 1d. above, the capital
value of £5,000, and is increased by 20 per cent.
in the case of absentee owners. A general assessment of all the lands in the Colony is made
triennially, each person's property in each district
or township being treated separately. The assess-
ments are then sorted alphabetically, in order to
discover the total holding of each individual which
is the basis upon which the higher or lower rate
of taxation is imposed. Little objection is taken
to the manner in which the value of the land is
assessed ; in the majority of cases the owner and
the official of the Government are able to agree as

3

to a fair valuation, and, should they fail to do so, an appeal against the valuation may be made to the Taxation Department, and, if an arrangement be not arrived at, to a Court of Law. The assessment of 1894 led to a large number of appeals, as the assessors had not realised the enormous fall in value of agricultural and pastoral land, but all, with a single exception, were met to the satisfaction of the appellant by concessions voluntarily made by the Department. Their attention is turned mainly to urban land, because it is subject to the greatest increase in unimproved value and returns the larger portion of the receipts derived from this source. An incidental advantage of the tax lies in the fact that land held by speculators for a rise in value contributes to the revenue equally with that on which buildings have been erected. The tax is recognised by most people as equitable in principle, but its progressive character has brought upon the Ministry the bitterest animosity of the landed class, who maintain that it has caused land to be given up and to become unsaleable, not so much because the present burden is intolerable but because it is merely the thin end of the wedge. They point to the programme of the Labour Party in which it is stated that the duty should be taken off certain articles of ordinary consumption, the deficiency (which, according to an official estimate, would be £310,000 a year) to be made up by increasing the tax on land values, and argue that as the Labour Party hold the

Government under their thumb, they will be able to enforce compliance with their wishes. It is difficult for a stranger to judge to what extent possessors of capital have actually been deterred from investing it in land, especially as several important factors have led concurrently to a depreciation in its value, such as the fall in the prices of wheat and wool, the failure of banks which were interested, directly or indirectly, in large tracts of country, and bad legislation, passed some ten years ago, under which the runs were cut up into blocks too small for the successful prosecution of the pastoral industry. The Government can point to Pastoral Acts which are admitted to be steps in the right direction, and challenge their opponents to show in what way they could have raised the £20,000 yielded by the additional Land Tax with less burden to the community. The Absentee Tax lacks similar justification, as it only brings in £3,600 a year. It is defended by the Premier on the ground that the absentee, as regards his property, has the full protection of the administration of the laws, and should contribute to the expenditure necessary for the maintenance of the State ; and that he does not do so to the extent of those who live in South Australia and contribute daily to the revenue by means of the Customs in all they eat and drink and practically all they put on. On the other hand it is contended that it is of supreme importance to attract capital to the Colony and that this principle is recognised in the case of public loans and Treasury bonds, on which no income tax is charged, and should also be taken into consideration with reference to private investments in land. Succession Duty is levied upon a graduated scale, ranging from $1\frac{1}{2}$ per cent. for £500 to 10 per cent. for £200,000 and upwards in the case of a widow, widower, ancestor or descendant of the deceased, and from 1 per cent. for any amount under £200 to 10 per cent. for £20,000 and upwards where the property is inherited by a person in any degree of collateral consanguinity. If the heir is a stranger in blood he pays 10 per cent. whatever be the value of the property. In order to promote the diffusion of wealth the rate of the tax is based upon the amount inherited, not upon the total value of the estate.

In the relief of the unemployed and the imposition of additional taxation, the Ministry, while choosing their methods, have dealt with problems which they were bound to face; but they have not confined themselves to the negative task of coping with existing difficulties. They have realised that greater commercial activity would permanently benefit the revenue and add to the demand for labour, and that, in a country like South Australia, it could only be secured by a wider and more varied cultivation of the soil, and have, with the hearty support of the Labour Party, seized every opportunity to encourage production and develop the export trade. Farmers already had the advantage of an Agricultural Bureau at Adelaide,

with local branches, which periodically disseminated
information, and of an Agricultural College to which
they could send their sons, at a small annual charge,
or gratuitously if they could obtain a scholarship ;
but they were hindered, when the fall in the value
of cereals compelled them to turn their attention to
subsidiary industries, by the absence of facilities for
obtaining a market for subsidiary products. The
limited demand in the Colony for butter, fruit, and
wine offered insufficient inducement to farmers and
small cultivators. Previous to 1893, the total export
of butter did not exceed the value of £1,200, but in
that year and in 1894 a bonus was offered by the
Government, with the result that butter of the value
of £110,000 has since been shipped. They also
formed a Produce Export Department through
which producers can ship their goods to London,
entered into a contract with the Peninsular and
Oriental and Orient Steamship Companies for cheap
rates of carriage, and established in London a Wine
and Produce Depôt to receive the goods and sell
them on the most favourable terms. A receiving
depôt has since been established at Port Adelaide
and refrigerating machinery and chambers have
been erected, which enable the Department to
receive sheep and send them as frozen meat to
England. Butter, wine, frozen meat, and fruit have
been sent to London through the Department, and
in some cases prices have been realised which far
surpassed those which could have been obtained in

the local market. The scheme is not yet self-supporting, as, though the charges cover the expenses, the salaries of the additional officials required in the Ministry, and an annual sum of some £3,500 for the maintenance of the Depôt in London, fall upon the revenue of the country ; but this expenditure is more than repaid by the impetus undoubtedly given to trade which would not otherwise have been afforded owing to the absence of private enterprise. The Ministry have undertaken a work in which individuals would have had little chance of success, and have enabled small consignors to ship their produce at wholesale rates. Their object also has been, in the words of the Minister of Agriculture (Dr. Cockburn), " to afford a guarantee of quality. All goods consigned to the Depôt are examined previous to shipment. If found to be in good condition and properly packed, they are sent forward to the London manager with a certificate to that effect. By this system of inspection a barrier is erected against the export of inferior goods which have an injurious effect on the reputation of South Australian produce." This latter point is of great importance and applies equally as regards the injury that might be done by one Province to another, as the British consumer regards Australian produce generically, and does not distinguish between the output of different Provinces. Dr. Cockburn called a conference in 1896, which was attended by representatives from New South

Wales, Victoria, and Queensland, to consider how
far joint action might be taken to secure uniformity
of output. The presence of a representative from
Victoria enhanced the practical character of the
deliberations, as that Province has been the pioneer
in the movement and conducts its operations on
a very extensive scale. It was decided that the
respective Parliaments should be invited to legislate
in the direction of uniform inspection of frozen
meat, dairy produce, wine and fruit, the adoption as
far as possible of a federal brand which would be
a guarantee of high quality and the joint exhibition
of Australian produce at some leading agricultural
show in England. The conference is regarded as
a promising sign of the willingness of the
Australian Provinces to act together in matters
of common concern. The institution of the
Produce Export Department is favourably viewed
by the press of South Australia and by the
bulk of the community, but, while it is admitted
that the initiative of the State has been successful, the hope is expressed that, when the trade
has been firmly established, the scope of State
action will be reduced and private enterprise be
allowed to step in. Such an attitude shows the
prevalent distrust of State action ; in order that it
may not be perpetuated, the middleman is to be
invited to absorb a portion of the profits which at
present are gained by the producer.

The present Ministry have also legislated on the

subject of workmen's liens, to protect the wage-earner against an insolvent or dishonest employer ; they have passed a Conciliation Act, to facilitate the settlement of industrial disputes, and have established a State Bank to provide for advances to farmers and other producers and to local authorities. These measures were warmly supported by the Labour members, who tried, unsuccessfully, to enlarge the scope of the State Bank by making it a Bank of Issue.

At the General Election in 1896 the Liberals, who were again successful, advocated certain measures of social reform ; continued economy of administration ; the extension of the functions of the Export Department ; Federation on a democratic basis, and the election of Ministries by Parliament, a proposal which has excited singularly little interest, in spite of the complete change that it would effect in the methods of government. The justification for it must be sought in the local conditions of the Province, which has never taken kindly to the system of government by party.

The tariff question, which has caused a clear line of division in New South Wales, has been settled decisively in favour of protection, and no distinct issue has taken its place at the recent elections. In Adelaide and the neighbourhood the contest may be said to have been fought in some sense between capital and labour, though among the supporters of the Ministry are many men of considerable means ;

or between individualism and socialism, but that all
are socialists to the extent of believing in State
ownership of railways and State control of waterworks and water conservation, while the majority
are favourably disposed to the Export Department,
and the average man has no definite ideas on the
subject, but views each proposed extension of State
action according to his opinion of its possible effect
upon himself. The success of the Liberals was
remarkable, as the South Australians are a fickle
people, and usually overthrow the party that is in
power ; but it is suggested that the female vote,
which has been given for the first time, may have
been recorded largely in favour of those who had
passed the Adult Suffrage Act. However that may
be, the Kingston Government are by no means sure
of an extension of three years, as the ties of party
allegiance are slight except in the case of the Labour
members, and the struggles in the Assembly may
resolve themselves, as in the past, into contests
between individual aspirants for office. The tendency of the last Parliament was in the direction of
a clearer line of cleavage, but this was due to the
cleverness of the present Premier, who included in
the Cabinet his two strongest opponents whose
opposition had been the more bitter that it was
not founded upon differences of political opinion.
Until that time South Australia had had forty-one
Ministries in thirty-seven years, a constant change
of the responsible heads of public departments

which greatly impaired their efficiency and prevented continuity of administration. The absence
of a stable majority in the Assembly gave the
opportunity, and ambition and love of power the
impetus, to continual struggles for office which
were wholly unallied with any baser motives, as
Australian statesmen have obtained an honourable
pre-eminence for their rectitude of character.

The intentions of the Government in regard to
the substitution of an elective executive, which have
not yet been definitely formulated, may be gathered
from a speech made by Dr. Cockburn, the principal
advocate of the change, in which he proposed that
Ministers, who would continue, as at present, to be
Members of Parliament, should be elected by ballot
by the Assembly at the commencement of each
session ; that they should appoint one of their
number to be their leader, but should be responsible individually to Parliament for their respective
departments ; and that their corporate responsibility
should be limited to matters affecting the Province
as a whole, such as finance or its relations with
other countries. The Governor's prerogative of
dissolution would remain unaffected, but as the
House would be brought into closer touch with
the people, dissolutions would be unnecessary
and undesirable. Dr. Cockburn claimed that his
proposal was in accordance with the natural evolution of Parliamentary Government, and contended
that, the area of selection being enlarged, the

best men would be chosen as Ministers from the whole House and the best man for each office. Ministers would not be called upon to justify proceedings of their colleagues which in their hearts they condemned, and private members would be able to exercise greater independence, as they would not be called upon to sacrifice their convictions to maintain their friends in office, and, being allowed greater freedom on questions of legislation, would introduce many bills of an important character. Intrigue, which was an essential of Party government, would become disreputable when resorted to for purposes of personal advancement. The objection that certain members would not work together if chosen to form an administration was met by the fact that men sat in amity on the Treasury benches who previously had denounced one another to the utmost of their power. The distinctive feature of the proposal, therefore, is the indirect election of Ministers. The people elect the representatives, who, in turn, are to elect certain of their number to form the Executive. The first criticism that suggests itself is, that it is difficult to believe in the rapid elimination of party feeling, and that it is probable, granted the existence of intrigues among aspirants for office under the present system, that they would be increased tenfold when such persons sought to ingratiate themselves, not only with prospective Premiers, but with a majority of the members of the Assembly. Again, while it is impossible to foresee all the results of the change, it may be anticipated that some obvious advantages would be counterbalanced by incoherence of policy and haphazard legislation, but that a class of men might be induced to come forward as candidates who are deterred by their horror of continual party strife. Dr. Cockburn stated that no amendment would be required in the Constitution Act, as, after the election of the Ministers, their names would be submitted in the ordinary way to the Governor. The present Ministry also favour the biennial retirement of half the members of the Assembly, in order to secure continuity in its composition, and the institution of the referendum.

These proposals are warmly supported by the Labour Party. They advocate elective Ministries on the ground that the people would obtain greater control over the Executive, that stability of government would be promoted, and that the legislative efficiency of Parliament would greatly be increased. They contrast the rapid dispatch of business by local governing bodies with the waste of time and obstruction which prevail in legislative assemblies. The biennial retirement of half the members of the Lower House commends itself to them for the reason which causes it to be opposed by men of conservative tendencies, that it would do away with the form of minority representation which is rendered possible in two-member constituencies by the widespread habit of plumping. They have

been foremost in their advocacy of the referendum
and the initiative, and one of their representatives,
Mr. Batchelor, has introduced a Bill which provides
for the establishment of the referendum, and contains the striking clause that " If petitions, signed
by not less than one-tenth of the electors entitled to
vote for the election of members of the House of
Assembly . . . . shall be presented to Parliament
praying that legislation shall be initiated on any
subject, the Attorney-General shall prepare, or cause
to be prepared, a Bill to give effect to such petition ;
and such Bill shall be introduced into Parliament as
a Government measure." Mr. Batchelor believes
that legislation would be accelerated on subjects
which fail to receive attention because Ministries
fear that they might alienate the sympathies of some
of their supporters.

The idea of the direct consultation of the people
upon a particular subject was put into practical
effect at the recent elections, when they were invited, in the form of an initiative, to say whether
they desired alterations in the law in regard to
education. Primary education in South Australia
is free, secular and compulsory. No religious instruction is permitted in the State schools, but the
Minister of Education has the power, on receiving
a written request from the parents of not less than
ten children who attend any school, to require the
teacher to read the Bible to any pupils who are
present for that purpose for half an hour before

half-past nine, the time at which the ordinary teaching commences. The direct reference to the people was the result of a Parliamentary resolution instigated by the advocates of denominational education, who contended that public opinion was veering round in their favour and believed that they would obtain a great accession of strength in the female vote which was to be exercised for the first time. It was couched in the form of the following questions, which were submitted to the electorate on a separate voting paper on the occasion of the general elections :—

1. Do you favour the continuance of the present system of education in the State schools ?

2. Do you favour the introduction of religious instruction in the State schools during school hours ?

3. Do you favour the payment of a Capitation Grant to denominational schools for secular results ?

The wording of the first and second questions was calculated to act in favour of the opponents of secularism, as the first would probably be answered in the negative not only by those who support religious instruction but also by many who believe that, in the present state of the finances, education should not be free except to such as are unable to pay for it. It was not made clear whether it was intended to apply to the system as a whole or merely to its secular character. The second question would bring together all who favour religious instruction, however much they may disagree among themselves as to the form in which it should be given. During the progress of the campaign the majority of the candidates declined to express their views upon the matter, but stated that they would be prepared to abide by the popular decision.

The following figures give the result of the reference for the whole Province with the exception of the Northern Territory, which has a very small electorate :—

1.	Yes ...	... 51,744.	No ...	... 17,755.
2.	Yes ...	... 18,889.	No ...	... 34,922.
3.	Yes ...	... 13,428.	No ...	... 41,975.

The classification of the papers is disappointingly meagre, as no information can be gathered as to the number of supporters of religious teaching and the capitation grant who were favourable to the other leading features of the existing system, nor as to the extent to which the friends of the capitation grant approved or disapproved of religious instruction in the State schools. The returns show, however, that, while 90,000 votes were given for Parliamentary candidates, some 20,000 persons either did not vote at all or gave an informal vote upon the distinct issue, and that less than one-fifth pronounced against the Act as it stands. The condemnation of the capitation grant is still more emphatic, and if the

supporters of religious teaching have less cause for
dissatisfaction, it may be noted that in no constituency were the affirmative in excess of the
negative replies, and that as the total number of
votes given upon the first question was far larger
than that on the second and third, thousands who
had voted affirmatively upon the first must have
considered that they had thereby returned a negative
reply to the others and should be reckoned as
additional opponents of religious instruction and
of the capitation grant. It is also noteworthy that,
contrary to the general expectation, the country
districts gave a considerably higher percentage of
votes in favour of the present system than the seven
constituencies which include Adelaide and its immediate neighbourhood. The advocates of religious
instruction have announced that they intend to
continue their efforts to win over the majority to
their views ; in the meanwhile, they will realise that
the process must be slow and will stir up the various
agencies of the churches to increased activity in a
sphere which is particularly their own.

The secular character of State education, which
dates from 1851, cannot be shown to have had evil
effects upon the conduct of the working classes, who
almost universally respect and obey the law and
have an air of confident independence which has
been fostered by manhood suffrage, high wages and
a high standard of comfort. South Australia was
fortunate in her original settlers, and has always

attracted a good class of immigrants. At present great benefit is accruing from the rapid development of Western Australia, which has relieved the pressure upon the labour market and increased the demand for South Australian goods. The latest Savings Bank returns give the total amount deposited as £2,713,000 and the number of depositors as 88,876, a very satisfactory rate for a population of about 320,000, especially when it is considered that the working classes also have large investments in Friendly and Building Societies. In conclusion, the visitor cannot but be struck by the entire absence of squalid poverty and of overcrowding in tenements and by the orderliness of the people and the high average of prosperity.

II

DEMOCRACY AND ITS SAFEGUARDS IN
NEW SOUTH WALES

The necessity for safeguards against financial extravagance and political pressure—The Crown Lands Act—The appointment of independent Railway Commissioners—The Standing Committee on Public Works—The Public Service Board—The unemployed, their numbers and treatment—The democratisation of the constitution—The Labour Party, its history, successes and aspirations.

THE inhabitants of New South Wales, as of several other Australian Provinces, lived for many years in a fool's paradise. They had received a magnificent inheritance in the land and were able, owing to the proved mineral resources of the country, to draw upon a practically inexhaustible fund in the willing advances of British capitalists. All classes vied with one another, especially in Victoria, in the extravagant loans and expenditure which caused the crisis of 1893, the greatest blessing, as many think, that has ever befallen Australia. Regardless of the burdens it was imposing upon future generations, the Parliament of New South Wales, with which I shall be dealing principally in the present chapter,

constructed unnecessary public works, allowed the
Civil Service to be packed with the friends and relations of those in power, and authorised roads and
bridges almost at the whim of each individual
member. This condition of things could not
continue indefinitely : on the one side, a rapidly
increasing debt, on the other, an enormous army
of civil servants, aspirants for employment on
public works and local claimants for a share of
the expenditure of loan funds, who were able,
on account of the wideness of the franchise and
the numerous functions undertaken by the Government, to bring pressure to bear upon the Ministry
through their representatives in the Assembly. It
was essential that the power to borrow should be
curtailed ; essential also that the possibilities of
political pressure should greatly be diminished.
The former object could only be achieved at
the cost of a comparative loss of credit, the latter
by a wise recognition on the part of the electorate
of the dangers of unfettered State action under a
democratic constitution.

The rapid growth of indebtedness cannot justly
be laid solely to the charge of the popular representatives, as, though the Legislative Council has occasionally resisted Loan Bills, it does not appear to
have realised the dangers of the proposed expenditure. Nor was it in human nature that it should
have opposed the construction of railways by which
its members, mostly landholders, would enormously

be benefited. Were their lands to be resumed by the
Government, they would obtain an enhanced price
for them ; in any case, many of them would gain a
large unearned increment. The members of the
Council who are nominated for life, similarly with
Labour members, lawyers, and others who represent
particular sections in Parliament, have been active
mainly where their own interests have been concerned. In pursuance of their right to reject
measures of taxation, they threw out Sir George
Dibbs' Income-Tax Bill in 1893 and, two years
later, Mr. Reid's Land and Income-Tax Assessment
Bill. As landholders they objected to a land tax,
and to an income tax as representatives of the
wealth of the community. Nor has the extravagance been due to payment of members, which is
regarded by some as the cause of all the evils of
Australia, as it was not inaugurated until after the
greater part of the indebtedness had been incurred ;
but the necessity for political safeguards has been
accentuated by the entrance into Parliament of
men who, owing to their pecuniary circumstances,
are less able to resist the demands of their electors,
are deeply interested in the postponement of dissolutions, and are more dependent upon their re-
election. It would be equally false to attach any
blame to the Labour Party, which did not make its
appearance in the Assembly until 1891.

While the great diminution of borrowing and consequently of the construction of public works has

lessened the opportunities for undue political influence, many still exist, and the number would
have been far greater in the absence of recent
legislation. How numerous these opportunities
might be, may be gauged from the fact that,
exclusive of some 10,000 railway employés,
20,000 persons were formerly in the service of
the State at an annual salary of £2,600,000; that
many thousands are tenants of the Crown, liable
to be propitiated by the reduction of their rent; that
nearly half the population live in unincorporated
districts, in which the local expenditure is met out
of national funds, and that the unemployed continually clamour for rations and employment upon relief
works, the receipt of which, under the existing law,
does not entail political disfranchisement.

The first legislative recognition of this danger is
seen in the Crown Lands Act of 1884, which constituted Local Land Boards, consisting of not more
than three members to be appointed by the Governor
in Council, which were to consider all applications
for land, insure the due fulfilment of the conditions,
residential or other, which are attached to different
forms of tenure, and appraise the rents of pastoral
leases and the rate of compensation for improvements. The practice of the Ministry has been to
appoint as chairman of a Board some experienced
official of the Crown Lands Department and, as his
colleagues, persons recommended by the residents in
the district. I am assured that this system of Land

Boards, whose decisions are subject to an appeal to the Land Court, has worked satisfactorily and that confidence has been promoted by the publicity of the proceedings. A full statement is published periodically, for each district, of the areas still open for settlement and of the conditions under which they can be taken up : the Land Boards have to inquire into the *bonâ fides* of the applicants. The question of the remission or suspension of the payment of rent is one of great difficulty in countries in which the Crown is the largest landholder. If a discretionary power is given to the Ministry, political pressure can be brought to bear upon them by tenants through their Parliamentary representatives ; if it be withheld, great hardship may ensue. This is particularly the case in Australia, where the value of a property may greatly be reduced by the devastations of rabbits or other pests and the consequent deterioration in the grazing capability of the land, or by a fall in the price which can be obtained for stock or wool. The Land Acts of New South Wales recognise either of the above causes as sufficient to entitle a pastoral lessee to a reappraisement of his rent by a Land Board, and permit the suspension of annual payments for one year in the case of holders of land under conditional purchase who reside upon it, but compel the vast majority of tenants of the Crown to abide strictly by the conditions of their agreements, under pain of the forfeiture of their holdings. Cases of individual hardship, which would engage the attentions of a private landlord, are, in the avoidance of a greater evil, left without redress.

In 1888 two further measures were passed with a similar object, the Government Railways and Public Works Acts. In a book recently published by authority of the Government,[1] to which I have to acknowledge my indebtedness, it is stated that the re-organisation of the railway administration was rendered necessary by the excess of political influence, the absence of expert control, and the construction of new lines without sufficient regard to the prospects of an early remunerative traffic, which had caused the capital expenditure to have been nearly doubled while the net earnings had not increased. Under the former Act, accordingly, the Government railways and tramways, which are now about 2,600 miles in extent and have been constructed at a cost of thirty-eight millions, were vested absolutely in a Board of three Railway Commissioners to be appointed by the Governor in Council. In order that their independence might be secured, they were made irremovable except for misbehaviour or incompetency, and then only upon a vote of both Houses, and their salaries were charged on the consolidated Revenue Fund, which was permanently appropriated to the required extent. They were entrusted with the general management of the railways and with the appoint-

[1] " New South Wales ; the Mother Colony of the Australias."

ment, subject to the regulations governing entrance into the public service, and dismissal, of all clerks, officers and employés, whose salaries and wages, however, are subject to the vote of Parliament. The Government were fortunate in securing the services of a very competent senior commissioner, who, with his colleagues, has been able, without lowering the rate of wages, to reduce the percentage of working expenses to gross revenue from 66·69 to 54·46 per cent., and has increased the net return on capital from 2·85 to 3·60 per cent. The result is the more satisfactory that the railways are not worked solely with a view to profit, but in such a manner as to benefit the population as a whole and to encourage the remote farmer and pastoralist. The experience of the other Australasian Provinces which established similar Boards proves it to be essential that the commissioners should not only possess great commercial ability, but be strong men who are able to withstand the pressure to which they will be subjected and are regardless of the attacks which are likely to follow upon their refusal of favours.

The Public Works Act provides for the appointment of a Parliamentary Standing Committee on Public Works, which is to consider and report upon all proposals for the construction of public works, except such as are connected with the military or naval defences of the Province, where the estimated cost exceeds £20,000, and upon any similar pro-

posals involving a smaller expenditure, which may
be submitted to it by the Governor in Council. It
consists of thirteen persons, eight members of the
Assembly and five of the Council, who are appointed
for the duration of a Parliament and receive remuneration at the rate of three guineas for each
sitting and thirty shillings a day for travelling expenses where the sittings are held at a distance from
Sydney. The Secretary for Public Works nominates
an equal number from both sides of the House after
consultation with the leader of the Opposition ;
in the majority of cases these nominations are
challenged and the appointments are made by
ballot of the whole House, which, according to
trustworthy information, leads to disreputable
negotiations between those who desire the additional salary and those who are able to confer it.

It has been suggested recently by a Royal Commission, which reported that " the expenditure on
public buildings is in excess of what is necessary,
owing to the system of political interference, which
is responsible for the erection of special post offices
in country townships where shops could be used,
and of costly courts of justice and other structures
which are not required," that all proposals for public
expenditure involving a probable outlay of more
than £5,000, should be considered and reported on
by a committee consisting of the permanent heads
of the Public Works Department, the Treasury, and
the Department on whose behalf the proposed ex-

penditure would occur. But the adoption of this suggestion would not go to the root of the evil, which lies in the manner in which small public works of a purely local character are carried out in rural districts. In the early days of the Province the Government, in order to widen the area of settlement, constructed all roads, bridges, and other local works out of national funds. As population increased, municipalities were established, which rated themselves for local purposes and received subsidies from the Government proportionately to the amounts thus raised; but the Act of 1867, which contemplated the extension of the system, provided that new municipalities, either boroughs or municipal districts, could only be created upon the receipt of a petition signed by a stated proportion of the prospective ratepayers. The Councils of such municipalities have the right to levy rates not exceeding two shillings in the pound in one year upon all rateable land within their borders, and receive from the Government during the first five years a sum equal to the whole amount actually raised in this manner or from any other specified source of revenue. This is gradually diminished until, at the end of fifteen years, no further subsidies are received, except such as have specially been voted by Parliament. At the present time, owing to the absence from the Act of any compulsory provision, the incorporated districts of the Province comprise somewhat more than half of the population, but less than one hundredth of the total area. Successive Governments have recognised the evil, but have failed to pass a satisfactory Amending Act which would establish some form of local government in the unincorporated areas and compel them to pay a fixed portion of their local expenditure. The estimates for such expenditure are framed by the Public Works Department, and are based upon the reports of its resident engineers and of the agents of the Government Architect. The opportunity of the pushing rural member occurs upon the expenditure of the unappropriated sum of money which is left in the hands of the Minister, to meet requirements that cannot be foreseen ; in this connection, members may threaten a withdrawal of their support and ministers may seek to win over new adherents. The reports of such actions are probably much exaggerated, as there are many who delight in vilifying the Assembly, but the popularity of a rural representative depends undeniably on the number of public works which the Government carry out in his district.

The next important step was the appointment, early in 1895, of a Royal Commission to inquire into the Civil Service, which reported that the Act of 1884, under which a Civil Service Board of five persons had been constituted, had failed in its purpose, because the Board consisted usually of men who had other duties to perform and had not the power to fix the salaries or control the service, and because the right was reserved to ministers in special cases to make appointments without either examination or probation. The Commissioners found that, owing to the absence of any well-ordered system of classification, the grossest inequalities and anomalies existed in the salaries of offices attached to different departments or even to the same department, as, to take an extreme case, that, in the department of the Government Architect the official who designed the Crown Lands office and supervised its erection was receiving less remuneration than the principal messenger; and that, while the service contained many high-minded and able officials, there were cases where incompetency, neglect of duty, and even drunkenness had formed no bar to continued employment. In accordance with their recommendations, founded on the belief that Parliament could not directly cope with the matter, an Act was passed in 1895 which constituted a Public Service Board of three persons, to be appointed for a period of seven years in the same way, and with the same securities for independence, as the Railway Commissioners. The Board was charged with the duty of making a thorough investigation, which was periodically to be repeated, into the working of each department, and of fixing the number, grade, and salary of the officials. Future appointments and promotions were to be made by the Governor in Council, upon a certificate of the Board, subject to the regulations in regard to competitive examinations and an obligatory period of probation upon entrance into the service. As the Commission had reported that it should be possible to effect an annual saving of a quarter of a million, special importance attached to the provisions which enabled the Board to dispense with the services of those who could not usefully and profitably be employed, such persons to receive gratuities on a fixed scale upon their retirement. The Board were sitting during my stay in Sydney and had to suffer from the open hostility of those who had been affected by their decisions and from abusive correspondence in the press. Their impartiality was impugned, and they were charged with allowing themselves to be influenced by the wishes of Ministers; but when the unpleasant task of retrenchment has been completed, they will doubtless carry on a work of practical utility unhampered by criticisms and accusations.

No serious attempt has yet been made to deal with the problem of the unemployed, which is the more urgent from the fact that the receipt of relief does not disfranchise the recipient. Its origin must be sought in the extensive Public Works policy of the past, which absorbed immigrants who would otherwise have settled on the land. In 1887 the majority of the great undertakings had been completed, and many thousand men, thus thrown out of employment, drifted into Sydney and led the Ministry to establish a   sual labour Board, which was discontinued after a year, but spent £252,000 in the relief of destitution. In the following years other causes intensified the distress : the great strikes of 1890 destroyed confidence and deterred enterprise ; the Broken Hill strike and the recent strike at Newcastle have had similar effects, the latter having struck a blow at the export trade in coal, which was gradually recovering from earlier disturbances ; the collapse of 1893 cast adrift a large number of mechanics and clerks whose services had been required during the period of inflation, the fall in the price of wool caused a shrinkage in private expenditure, and the severe drought experienced during the latter part of 1895 had disastrous effects on the labours of those employed in mining, pastoral, and agricultural pursuits. To meet the difficulty a Labour Bureau was established at Sydney in 1892, in order that the unemployed might be able to register themselves and might be helped to obtain work ; but, while much has been done in this direction, no more satisfactory solution has been found for the problem, as a whole, than continual relief works, which attract the destitute from country districts and other Provinces, and afford merely temporary alleviation of the distress. According to a recent report of the Superintendent of the Bureau, to whom I am indebted for information, £201,000 were spent during the year ending February last (in a population of a million and a quarter) upon works in

aid of the unemployed, an expenditure of which
two items alone, £50,000 for forest thinning and
£35,000 for railway deviations, can be supposed to
have had any other justification. Mr. Creer told
me in June, 1896, that the daily attendance at the
Bureau had averaged for several months 1,500 to
2,500, but had decreased latterly to 300 to 500 ;
that many who had been given employment had
abandoned it, and that, where a large number had
been working together, he had had much trouble
owing to their rowdiness and bad behaviour. On
this point the Premier, Mr. Reid, stated that he
had been informed, on good authority, that there
were not more than 1,500 genuine unemployed in
Sydney, but admitted, quoting his informant, that
"there are also hundreds of men who do little or
no work" and "a large number of men who have
been identified with the unemployed agitation for
the past ten years, and who appear to delight in its
existence, as no doubt they consider it a capital
cover to pose as *bonâ-fide* workmen out of employment." The conduct of the latter is mainly due to
the weakness of successive Ministries, which have
failed to resist pressure and may almost be said to
have encouraged idleness. Such encouragement is
also provided in the climate of Sydney, which enables
men to sleep in the open for nine months of the
year without discomfort. Mr. Creer proposed that
those who profess to be willing to work should be
employed upon schemes of water conservation and

irrigation in the drier parts of the Province, which should be carried out by gangs of men under strict supervision, and that the confirmed loafers should be placed in Industrial Homes and be compelled to choose between work and starvation. The present Government have established thirty-five branches of the Labour Bureau, which will tend to prevent the unemployed from flocking into the Metropolis. But the bulk of the unemployed at Sydney are demoralised by idleness and ignorant of agricultural pursuits, and can only be dealt with by a strong Minister who, regardless of political consequences, will discontinue the system of indiscriminate relief and treat the confirmed loafers with the greatest severity.

Democratic government, actively opposed by some and detested by most of the more educated members of the community, is firmly established in New South Wales, and is essential to the happiness of the people there as elsewhere in Australasia, in the general prevalence of purely commercial instincts and the absence of a landed class which is bound by inherited traditions to take an interest in its dependents. Of recent years the democratic movement has been more rapid : payment of Members of the Assembly dates from 1889, Sir George Dibbs passed manhood suffrage in 1893, and Mr. Reid seeks to curtail the power of the Upper House. A great impetus has been given by the Labour members, whose numbers and influence entitle them to be regarded as one of the most important political factors in the Province. The reason for the formation of a separate party has thus been explained to me by one of its members : the prominent men among the working classes, who were anxious to promote progressive legislation, were hampered by the fact that they disagreed upon the question of the tariff, and that their votes were, consequently, useless as far as the advancement of such legislation was concerned. The line of cleavage in the Assembly was between Protectionists and Free Traders ; reactionary and advanced views were represented on both sides of the House. They felt, therefore, that labour would be powerless unless the issue of the tariff were explicitly sunk and a programme put forward which would concentrate the votes of the working classes. In their campaign they were doubtless aided by the Act passed for the payment of members, and by the failure of the maritime and other strikes, which impressed Trades Unionists with the necessity of seeking to attain their ends by other means. A programme was, accordingly, drawn up, of which the principal items were, in order of importance, Electoral Reform, the Right of Mining for Gold on Private Land, and the Taxation of Land Values ; it was adopted at the elections of 1891 by a large number of candidates who came forward in the Labour interest and succeeded in winning thirty-four seats. Upon the meeting of

Parliament it was decided by the Party, although
the majority had Protectionist leanings, that
support should be accorded to Sir H. Parkes, who
had made Electoral Reform the principal item of
his policy. A few months later he was defeated on
the Coal Mines Regulation Bill, and the votes of
the Labour Party were transferred to his Protectionist successor, Sir G. Dibbs, who also favoured
Electoral Reform ; but, in the meanwhile and subsequently, many of the Labour members refused to
leave their views on the tariff in abeyance, with
the result that the number of those who adhered
staunchly to the programme was reduced to five or
six. In spite of these defections, the first two items
in the programme were carried and the Taxation of
Land Values took the foremost place. At the 1894
elections the Labour Party had been much discredited, but secured fifteen representatives, in
the Assembly of one hundred and twenty-five,
who were pledged to the so-called "solidarity"
vote. Their support was then transferred to Mr.
Reid, the present Free Trade Premier, who was in
favour of the Land Tax, which they enabled him to
carry in 1895, though only after a further election,
caused by the action of the Upper House, at which
they carried three additional seats. At present the
Labour Party are concentrating all their efforts
upon the abolition of the Legislative Council and
the substitution for it of the referendum, which they
regard as a necessary preliminary to the passage of

advanced legislation, and are prepared to accept, as
a step in the right direction, Mr. Reid's proposal
that the tenure of the members of the Council who
are nominated for life should be reduced to a
period of years, and that all-important Bills, upon
which the Assembly and Council have failed to
agree in two consecutive sessions, should be
referred to a plebiscite. They argue that when
the electors realise that the Council can only delay
legislation for one session, and that the issue is then
directly referred to them, they will sweep it away as
a mere obstacle in the path of progress. It may
be doubted whether the adoption of the plebiscite
would have the results that they anticipate, but it
cannot be doubted that a compact body of representatives, aiming at the democratisation of the
constitution and willing to support whichever party
makes the highest bid for their votes, have but to
remain united to achieve their object, especially
when it is in accordance with the natural evolution
of Parliamentary government. The Labour members have a definite programme upon which all
their efforts are concentrated, but are chary of
giving their views upon other questions, as their
votes, in consequence of the common pledge, will
depend on the decision of the majority of the party.
Great indignation is expressed at the "caucus"
meetings, at which the votes of all are thus determined ; but it is difficult to see wherein the conduct of the Labour members differs essentially

from that of the representatives who support one of the principal parties in the State. In both cases certain main objects are sought and individual convictions are, on occasion, subordinated to their attainment ; the only difference is that, in the latter case, the action is taken voluntarily in order to maintain a party in power ; in the former, its expediency is determined by the majority of those who are united in a common purpose. On the other hand it must be admitted that the Labour Party display, at present, all the irresponsibility of independence, and have often acted in such a manner as to justify the hostility of their opponents. During my stay at Sydney they attempted, on one occasion, to convert the Assembly into a court of judicial appeal ; on another, to interfere with the actuarial calculations of insurance societies.

The importance of political safeguards is accentuated not only by the accelerated movement in the direction of constitutional change, but by the increasing belief in the efficacy of State control and state interference. During the session of 1896 the Government brought forward measures dealing with the conservation of water, the public health, adulteration, and the regulation of coal mines and of factories and workshops, the passage of which would necessitate a considerable increase in the number of State officials ; and the Labour Party, the transference of whose support would place the Ministry in danger of defeat, have shown, by their votes in the past, their conviction that all new public works which are in the nature of a monopoly, should be constructed and owned by the State.

The scope of my inquiries in New South Wales led me in directions which have caused me to emphasise the darker sides of political life; but I wish to guard against the inference that similar shadows could not have been found elsewhere, and have touched upon the subject in my general observations upon Australasian tendencies. In fact, I may add, I was drawn into my particular line of study at Sydney by the knowledge that New South Wales had taken especial precautions, except in regard to the unemployed, against the evils which I have here sought to summarise. The predominant note in that Province is one of hopefulness : the vast pastoral, mineral, agricultural, and other resources of the country, the harbour at Sydney which renders it the natural centre of the foreign trade of the Continent, and the rapidity of the recovery from the crisis of 1893, are calculated to inspire confidence in the future; as are the high average wages of the working classes, the low cost of living, and the short hours of labour. But the most impressive sign of a healthy national life is the readiness of the democracy to recognise the dangers inherent in its rule, and to divest itself voluntarily of some of its powers, in the interests of pure and upright government.

III

PROBLEMS OF QUEENSLAND

The agitation of Central and Northern Queensland for separation from the South—The " Kanaka " traffic—White and coloured labour on the plantations—The Sugar Works Guarantee Act—The irregularity of employment in the sugar and pastoral industries—The conditions and opinions of the shearers—Assistance to dairymen and producers of frozen meat—The Labour Party, its history and prospects — Criticisms of the Government—The principles of State action.

IN the Southern Provinces of Australia, Sydney, Melbourne and Adelaide are not only the political capitals, but have become naturally, from their geographical position and other advantages, the points of departure of the trunk lines of railway and the centres of commercial and intellectual activity. In the case of Queensland, Brisbane, which was selected as the capital because settlement was almost confined to its neighbourhood, had to compete with several other good harbours ; it is situated at the south-eastern extremity of a vast territory, and is connected only by sea with the northern parts above Bundaberg. The existence of this means of communication caused successive Governments to

postpone the construction of a coastal railway in
favour of lines running from East to West which
would promote the development of the pastoral
resources of the interior by affording access to the
nearest port ; but these lines, which start from
Brisbane, Rockhampton, and Townsville, and have
a respective length of 483, 424, and 235 miles, have
tended, by increasing the importance of the latter
places, to foster in their inhabitants a feeling of
jealousy at the supremacy of the former and of
antagonism of interests with the South. The
climatic conditions also are divergent : the Centre
and South are semi-tropical ; the North, which lies
wholly within the tropics, contains a low fringe of
fertile land along the coast, suitable for the cultivation of sugar, and the cause of the constant struggles
which have surrounded the question of the employment of coloured labour.

The establishment of Queensland as a separate
Province dates from 1859, and was at once followed
by an extension of population to the Northern
districts, and a few years later by the growth of a
demand for separation, which culminated in 1871 in
a petition to the Crown, in which the desire was expressed that the country to the North of the Dawes
Range, which lies between Gladstone and Bundaberg,
should be created into a new Province, on the
ground that the absence of regular communication
between the capital and the Northern settlements
rendered good government and the administration

of justice very difficult and uncertain. During the
succeeding years the agitation flickered in the North
and was latent in the Centre, which had been conciliated by the construction of its railways and
appeared to have identified itself with the South.
Some ten years ago the Northern members pressed
their claims very strongly, and more recently the
Central members have petitioned the Crown, sent a
deputation to the Colonial Secretary, and brought
their case before the Queensland Parliament.

The arguments advanced by the Northern and
Central separationists are similar in character, and
if recognised as valid in the case of the Centre, must
be doubly so when applied to the North, owing to
its greater distance from the capital and the difficulty
of communication with many of its outlying districts. The boundaries adopted by the separationists
are those laid down by the Real Property (Local
Registries) Act of 1887, under which the Province
was divided into three parts, of which the Northern
contains 255,000, the Central 223,000, and the
Southern 190,000 square miles.

The claims of the Centre, to which I have been
able to give more attention, as I spent some time in
that district, are based not only upon alleged unjust
apportionment of expenditure, defective administration, and financial hardships endured under the
protective tariff for the benefit of Southern manufacturers, but upon the inherent and inalienable
right of a community of free British people. It is

pointed out that Central Queensland is in a more advanced position than were Victoria and Queensland at the time of their separation from New South Wales ; that it returns less members than the city of Brisbane and the country within a radius of ten miles of it ; and that the Northern and Central members, even if unanimous in favour of separation, would only number twenty-seven as against the forty-five representatives of the South, and are bound, apart from the constitutional aspect of the question, to look to the intervention of the Imperial Government. The most important utterance from this source is the reply of Sir Henry Holland, now Lord Knutsford, to the Northern deputation, in the course of which he said that "there is no instance of recent years, since the Colonies attained the greatness they have, of the Imperial Legislature passing an Act interfering with the administration of one of those great Colonies, except at the request of the Colonial Government. Therefore I say it is difficult, if not undesirable, to deal with such a question as this unless we have the authority, on a desire expressed on the part of the Colonial Legislature, or unless there is some case made out which is absolutely overwhelming ; " and Mr. Chamberlain recently stated, with reference to Central separation, that, even if local agreement had been reached, the difficulties and risks attending any attempt to divide the Province were, under existing circumstances, very great. He clearly appreciated the hostile feeling that would be aroused throughout

Australia by any interference on the part of the Imperial Authorities with the internal government of an Australian Province. As the separationists do not hope to obtain a majority in the Queensland Assembly, they are likely to be ardent advocates of Federation, especially if a clause be inserted in the Constitution which would enable the Federal Government to subdivide a Province without the consent of its Parliament.

The Southern members are influenced by the fear that, under separation, they would lose the Northern and Central markets. To meet this objection, a resolution was moved in the Assembly by one of the members for Rockhampton that the separation of Central Queensland was desirable, but on such terms that the interchange of natural products between the two Provinces should continue to be free from tax or duty; but the proposal, which was seen to be fraught with endless difficulties, has not been regarded seriously. The question has also arisen in what manner the liability for the public debt would be distributed in the case of separation, but it is contended that the matter would be settled under the Imperial Act of 1861, under which both Provinces would jointly be liable for the whole debt, and machinery is provided for arbitration as to the proportion of it which would be borne by each of the Provinces.

The necessity for some form of decentralisation has been recognised, and partially acted on, by

successive Ministries since 1877, when a Royal
Commission was appointed to inquire into the
best means of bringing about a more equitable
distribution of the revenue. The system of Local
Government, introduced in 1878 and extended in
the following year to rural districts, lessened the
direct control exercised from Brisbane, and handed
over to elective Municipal Councils and Divisional
Boards the expenditure of the revenue raised for
local purposes. In 1887 local registries of titles to
real estate were established at Townsville and Rockhampton, and Sir S. Griffiths introduced a Financial
Districts Bill, to divide the Province into three districts and to provide for separate accounts of revenue
and expenditure. The Bill was not passed, but
separate returns have since been published, which
do not, however, give a full statement of the contributions of the different districts to the revenue.
In 1892 the same Minister introduced a Constitution
Bill, in which he proposed to place Queensland
under a federal system of Government, a General
Assembly of the United Provinces, and three Provincial Parliaments. In the course of discussion
the number of Provinces was reduced from three to
two, to the exclusion of the Centre, which was to
retain its connection with the South. The Bill
passed the Assembly, and was thrown out by the
Council, principally on the ground that it had not
been supported by the statutory two-thirds majority.
The Central Separationists were naturally opposed

to the Bill in its amended form, and public opinion
in the North was equally hostile. It was pointed
out that the expenses of government would greatly
be increased, even more than under territorial
separation, and that the powers of the Provincial
Parliament would be so limited, in the absence of
control over the railways and the customs tariff,
that the North would not enjoy the enhanced
prosperity which, under an entirely separate
Government, would make it indifferent to the
additional expenditure. The appointment of a
judge of the Supreme Court to reside at Townsville, and, since last year, at Rockhampton, has
lessened the expenditure and loss of time involved
in legal proceedings initiated in the Northern and
Central Districts. In the Ministerial measure
dealing with the election of delegates to represent
Queensland at the Australian Federal Convention,
which failed to become law owing to an insoluble
deadlock between the two Houses, it was proposed
that, of the ten delegates, three should be elected by
the Northern and two by the Central Parliamentary
Representatives, a greater proportion than would be
warranted by their respective populations as compared with that of the South. The Premier, Sir Hugh
Nelson, defended the liberality of this proposal on
the ground that "it is of the utmost importance that
in any federal constitution provision should be made
for the division of existing Colonies and the terms
on which such divisions shall take place ; " adding

that "the Northern and Central districts have a perfectly legitimate aspiration : they are looking forward to the day when they will be formed into separate states."

The above remarks embody the views of many South Queenslanders who look forward to eventual separation, but are not prepared to advocate it at present ; the Central separationists, on the other hand, contend that the question is ripe for immediate settlement, and, as a proof of popular feeling in the matter, point out that ten out of the eleven representatives of Central Queensland are pledged to separation, and that numerous petitions were handed to the late Governor, Sir Henry Norman, on the occasion of his tour through the district. Personal observation and inquiries directed to all with whom I came in contact, have convinced me that the enthusiasm for separation is greatly on the wane in the Centre, owing to the strength of the Labour Party, which, in 1896, carried a majority of the Central seats, and to the inevitable reaction which succeeds a period of excitement. The owners of property and tradespeople of Rockhampton have everything to gain by a change which would make their town the capital of a province ; the miners at Mount Morgan and the shearers are indifferent, though the latter, judging from a conversation which I had with some twenty of them, have a vague idea that under separation the Labour Party, of which they are supporters, would be in a stronger position ; and the pastoralists, who

direct the principal industry of the community, are
practically unanimous in their opposition : they have
obtained the railway which has opened up the
Western Downs, and they dread the predominance
of the Labour Party and of Rockhampton, the
inhabitants of which, they maintain, have shown
little regard for their interests.

As regards the feeling in the North, I have been
told by one of the Northern members, himself a
supporter of separation, and by others, that the
agitation is at present dormant. The election of
local men has been promoted by the payment of
members ; previously most of the Northern representatives were inhabitants of Brisbane, who were
out of touch with the feelings and interests of their
constituents. Material and political considerations
also have exercised great influence. The sugar
planters, ardent advocates of separation as long as
the importation of coloured labour was forbidden,
have been staunch supporters of the Union since
the removal of the prohibition and the passage of
the Sugar Works Guarantee Act. On the other
side, the Labour Party, who share in the hatred
of coloured labour which is common to the
working classes throughout Australasia, opposed
separation while it was likely to lead to its legalisa-
tion, but have been encouraged by their present
strength, the tenure of seven seats out of sixteen
in the Northern district, in the belief that, if they
obtained separation, they might hope again to

exclude it, and would have an opportunity of giving effect to their general political views.

The "Kanaka" question has been so fully discussed in the press and in numerous pamphlets, that the Imperial and Provincial Acts, which first aimed at the protection of the islanders, may be dismissed with the remark that they are admitted in Queensland to have had abundant justification. The conditions have been made successively more stringent until, at the present time, it is almost impossible that any Kanakas should be taken against their will, ill-treated on the voyage, or oppressed upon the plantations. Government agents, to give a brief summary of the Acts, accompany all recruiting vessels and are bound to see that the islanders understand the nature of the agreement into which they are about to enter, as to rate of payment, and duration of service ; that every return passenger is duly landed along with his property at his own village or district, and that the islanders receive the prescribed provisions and clothing on the journey, and are otherwise treated in accordance with the regulations. Inspectors receive the vessels upon their arrival in Queensland, superintend the signature of the agreements, and, generally, are responsible for the welfare of the labourers during their residence in the country. In the case of sickness employers are bound to provide proper medicine and medical attendance, and they may be called upon to contribute towards the maintenance of a hospital.

The contentment of the labourers may be inferred
from the fact that a large proportion re-engage
themselves upon the expiration of the term of three
years, and that, of the 1,305 who were landed during
the year 1895, 250 had previously been employed in
Queensland. As the result of frequent intercourse,
the conditions are well known in most of the islands
from which the labourers are recruited. According
to official figures, the number of islanders in Queensland increased in 1895 from 7,853 to 8,163, of whom
nearly two-thirds are in the districts of Mackay and
Bundaberg ; all are employed on the cultivation of
sugar, with the exception of a few at Thursday
Island, who are engaged in the bêche-de-mer and
pearl-shell fisheries.

It would seem that the only valid objection which
can now be made against the system, except by
those who disagree from the whole thing on
principle, is, that it may lead to the gradual de-
population of some of the islands by the withdrawal
of a considerable proportion of the adult males of
marriageable age. It may be noted, in this connection, that the islanders have also been recruited for
Guatemala, if not for other countries.

The mode of cultivation and the treatment of the
raw material have been modified during the last few
years. At first the cane was grown solely in large
plantations, each of which possessed a separate mill
and treated only its own produce ; but as prices fell
and the local demand was overtaken, more scientific

methods began to prevail. It was found, on the one
hand, that the cane could be treated most economically on a large scale ; on the other, that few plantations were sufficiently extensive to keep a large mill
at work during the whole season. To meet these
conditions, central mills were constructed and the
land was in many cases subdivided, and let or sold
on a system of deferred payments to farmers, who
were encouraged to cultivate it in small areas, and
to send their cane to the factories. The interests of
the mill-owner and the farmers should be identical ;
the former is anxious that his mill should be worked
to its full capacity, and has every inducement to
dispose of his land upon terms favourable to cultivators ; the latter have a sure outlet for the disposal
of their produce. In 1894, fully 40 per cent. of the
80,000 acres under cane was cultivated in areas of
ninety acres and under. An impetus was given to
this movement by the temporary prohibition of the
importation of islanders, which compelled planters to
consider the possibility of an alternative to coloured
labour, and by a vote of £50,000, by means of which
two central mills were erected for groups of small
farmers. The success of these mills induced the
Government to pass the Sugar Works Guarantee
Act, under which " any company which can give
the Government security in land, has the requisite
cane crops growing for a fair season's mill work,
and can show that it has an area of land capable of
supplying the mill with a full crop, can obtain the

sanction of the Government to accept a tender for the erection of a factory, the State guaranteeing the interest and the redemption of the debentures issued in payment for it. By this measure the country has not only supplied the means for the steady development of the industry, but has taken, in its belief in the soundness of the enterprise, a direct interest in it. No surer guarantee can exist than this law, that the Parliament of Queensland will in future safeguard the prosperity of an undertaking in which the State has so keen an incentive to protect itself from loss."[1] The contingent liability incurred by the State in the year ending June, 1895, was £157,000, and in the preceding year £44,000 : the amount is likely to be increased, as the construction of seven additional mills has been conditionally approved of, but, under an amending Act of 1895, is not to exceed a total of £500,000. The Premier sees no reason to suppose that, with proper management, any of the new factories will fail to meet their liabilities to the State.

Under these circumstances the question arises whether coloured labour will permanently be necessary, the answer to which depends upon the ability of the white man to become acclimatised in a tropical country. "If the white man," to quote a prominent Queenslander, "can live and work and bring

---

[1] Quoted, by permission of the author, from an article contributed to the *Australasian Review of Reviews* by Mr. J. V. Chataway, one of the members for Mackay.

up his children in the tropics of this continent, then assuredly the time will come when we shall require coloured labourers to cultivate our cane no more than do the continental sugar-beet farmers require coloured men to do their field work. Where can we look for proof of the European's ability to work and live in the heated North ? He works on railways and in mines now, but there is an entire lack of evidence that his children and his children's children can continue to do so with unimpaired health and vigour. Again, it has to be seen what will be the normal death-rate in the North. It has been heavy, but we have yet to estimate the lowering of that rate as the malarial swamps are drained, and the dense tropical scrubs cleared away. . . . Time alone can solve this question thoroughly, though it may be permitted one to say that so far there is ample reason to think that the evidence is accumulating in favour of the European's ability to permanently inhabit and cultivate our tropical lands. There is some satisfaction in noting, for instance, that, despite the increased settlement in Northern Queensland, the death-rate for the Colony has fallen from 22·97 per 1,000 in 1884 to 12·08 in 1894."[1] The rate of mortality among the Kanakas is reported officially to have been 40·62 per 1,000 in 1894, and 29·64 in 1895. Their employment is absolutely prohibited in the mills, and is restricted to certain forms of work upon the plantations. The Govern-

[1] See footnote p. 66.

ment are anxious to replace the Kanakas gradually by white labourers and to settle the tropical littoral with a population of small farmers. This object, however, it is contended, cannot be attained without the temporary employment of coloured labour. Another aspect of the question may be noted : granted that white men cannot at present do all the work upon the plantations, Kanakas are preferable to Orientals, whether Chinese or Japanese, who would remain permanently in the country. Even in Queensland, though less than in the Southern Provinces, such a state of things would be regarded as eminently undesirable.

A considerable demand for white labour has thus been created, the extent of which may be gauged from the figures given to me by a planter who has 3,000 acres under cane in the neighbourhood of Bundaberg. Upon land which formerly carried 800 head of cattle and gave employment to a single married couple, he now employs 300 Kanakas and 80 white men during the whole of the year, and 120 additional white men during the crushing season, which lasts, as a rule, from June to December. The latter are compelled to shift for themselves during the remaining months of the year and wander about the country in the search for casual work ; many, it is said, seek it in the agricultural districts of the Darling Downs.

The people of Queensland are confronted with a serious problem in the fact that of the three

principal industries of the countries, mining alone
affords regular and constant employment, and that
only on proved goldfields. In the sugar industry,
as stated, about 40 per cent. of the labourers, exclusive of the islanders, are permanently employed,
and in the pastoral industry the proportion is even
smaller. On a typical sheep-station in the Central
district which carries 80,000 sheep, the permanent
staff number only 19, and are supplemented at
shearing time by some 25 to 30 shearers and as
many more workmen who pick up, sort, and pack
the fleeces. The shearers with whom I conversed
bewailed the irregularity of their employment; they
work at high pressure for a few months in the woolsheds, and have no fixed occupation during the
remainder of the year. I was favourably impressed
by the men, and was informed that, as a class, they
have much improved of late years, and that many
of them have considerable savings. Allowances must
be made for workmen who are herded together,
good characters with bad, and lead a nomadic and
demoralising existence which lacks the sobering
influences of sustained industry and domestic associations. Recent Ministries have been alive to
the importance of this question and have aimed
at the gradual diminution of the size of pastoral
properties held from the Crown. The Land Act of
1884 divided them into two equal parts, over one of
which the holder was offered a fixed lease for 21
years, while the other was to be subject to resump-

tion by the State as the demand for the land might arise. Under this provision large tracts of country have been thrown open for occupation as grazing farms of from 5,000 to 20,000 acres and have been eagerly taken up, as many as twenty applications having been received for a single farm where the quality of the soil has been exceptionally favourable. The Act of 1894, passed by the present Government, established a new form of tenure which was intended to meet the special requirements of the shearers. Grazing homesteads not exceeding 2,500 acres in area may be acquired at a low rental, subject to the condition that the selector must reside upon the land for not less than six consecutive months in each year during the first ten years of his lease ; but, under license from the Land Board, the selectors of two or more homesteads may co-operate to work their holdings as a whole, in which case residence by one-half of the whole number of selectors will fulfil the conditions of occupation. Some of the shearers may, from the force of habit, be incapable of a settled existence ; but many of them proclaim their desire to occupy land and are hereby afforded an opportunity which they have scarcely at present realised. The attractiveness of this form of tenure will be increased if the Government pass their proposed legislation to authorise them to sink bores for the supply of water to the smaller holdings.

A better state of things prevails upon the Darling Downs in the south of the Province, where the shearing is done by cultivators and others who are in regular employment. This part of the country should eventually carry a large resident population engaged in the growth of cereals and in dairy-farming. To promote settlement and "in the strong belief that Queensland is capable of and will soon be supplying not only her own requirements, but also of exporting largely of her surplus farm products, the Government have made provision in connection with the Torres Strait Service for the carriage of farm and dairy produce in large quantities, and have also submitted to Parliament a measure for the appointment of an additional Minister, to be charged solely with the development of agricultural interests, and have taken the necessary steps for the establishment of an agricultural college within a reasonable distance from Brisbane."[1] The export of dairy produce has been encouraged by the offer of a bonus, and the construction of butter factories by loans, the funds being obtained from a portion of the proceeds of a tax imposed upon owners of sheep and cattle by the Meat and Dairy Produce Encouragement Act of 1893. The remainder is expended in advances to proprietors of meat works, and it is provided in a subsequent Act, that the amounts received in payment of interest or repayment of the principal of the loans, may be refunded to the payers of the tax. The progress of settlement has been retarded by the alienation from

[1] Financial statement 1896, p. 14.

the Crown of much of the land that is most suitable for the purpose, both in quality and situation. The freehold has in many cases passed to financial institutions, which, having advanced upon it an amount greater than the present value as depreciated by the fall in prices, are unwilling to sell the land and to reconcile themselves to their losses. The Government have been authorised by the Agricultural Land Purchase Act of 1894, to expend a sum not exceeding £100,000 a year in the purchase, under voluntary agreement, of land suitable for agricultural settlement which is to be offered for selection in agricultural farms, and have made considerable use of their powers, but the system has not been sufficiently long in operation to enable an estimate to be formed of its results.

The irregularity of employment has engendered among the working classes a widespread feeling of discontentment, and constitutes one of the main causes of the numerical strength of the Labour vote, which amounts to about 34 per cent. of the whole. The Parliamentary Labour Party in Queensland differs from that of the other Australian Colonies in its close identification with directly socialistic aspirations. It was founded to give effect to the political platform of the Australian Labour Federation, published in 1890 under the influence of the communist, William Lane, which advocates "the nationalisation of all sources of wealth and all means of producing and exchanging wealth;"

its organ, *The Worker*, writes under the motto "Socialism in our time," and several of its members publicly admit that they are Socialists. Others, however, who look forward to the possibility of an alliance with a reconstructed Opposition ask to be judged solely by the programme of the party which contains no distinctly socialistic item, in the popular acceptation of the term, except the establishment of a State Labour Department to which men may apply as a right for work at a minimum wage ; but they will have difficulty in overcoming the general impression, which their opponents, not unnaturally, do all in their power to intensify.

The Party first came into prominence at the elections in 1893, when they won fifteen seats out of seventy-two, and have nothing to show in the way of practical legislation to counterbalance the undoubted consolidation of the forces of their opponents. A comparison suggests itself with the success of the Labour Parties in New Zealand and South Australia which have co-operated with progressive Ministers in the enactment of measures of social reform. In the latter case, the Labour Party have been so moderate in their programme, speeches, and actions, that they have carried a quarter of the seats in the Legislative Council, and thus prove themselves not to have alienated the householders and small owners of property who form the bulk of the electorate for that House. In New South Wales

the Labour Party have been able, by opportunistic
transfers of their votes, to secure electoral reform
and the taxation of incomes and land values. The
position of affairs in Queensland is not analogous ;
the coalition of Sir S. Griffith and Sir T. McIlwraith
practically destroyed the Opposition, and made it
necessary for the Labour Party to trust almost
entirely to their own efforts, which should have
been directed towards the concentration of all the
progressive feeling of the community. Their policy,
on the contrary, has deprived them of the support
of many who are dissatisfied with the Government,
and has not materially strengthened their hold upon
the working classes. Though they carried twenty
seats in 1896, they only polled 964 more votes than
in 1893, nor have they improved their position in
the House, as, even should they be supported by the
ten Oppositionists and Independents, they would be
confronted by a solid phalanx of forty-two Ministerialists. It may be of interest to note that their
principal successes have been gained among bush-
men and miners, but that they also hold the sugar
district of Bundaberg, two agricultural constituencies, two seats at Rockhampton, and three
in the poorer and outlying parts of Brisbane.

The complaints of the Labour Party against the
Government were directed mainly to their failure to
amend the electoral laws or to pass humanitarian
legislation, and to the stringency of the Peace
Preservation Act of 1894. Apart from their obvious

objections to the plural vote of persons holding
property in different divisions, they contend that
many miners and shearers are permanently dis-
franchised, as they are neither householders nor
reside for six months in the same place, and that
persons qualified to be registered are impeded by
the provisions which oblige them to fill in a claim
in which, among other things, they have to state
their qualification, and to get the claim attested by
a justice of the peace, electoral registrar, or head
male teacher of a State school. The Peace
Preservation Act was passed at a time when a
serious disturbance had arisen from a strike of
shearers in the pastoral districts of the West, on
the ground that the ordinary laws of the Colony
were insufficient for the prevention, detection, and
punishment of crime in such districts, and was as
strongly justified by some as it was condemned
by others. The Act authorised the Executive to
proclaim districts which should come under its
operation, and to appoint such district magistrates
as might be necessary for carrying its provisions
into effect. These may be summarised in the
words of the Hon. T. J. Byrnes, the Attorney-
General : " The first portion of this legislation is to
give us power to put an end to the carrying of arms
and the sale of arms in the districts that have been
disturbed . . . It is proposed in the second part of
the Bill that inquests on crime may be held . . .
The third portion of the Bill deals with the power

of arrest and detention of persons under suspicion."
Under the latter heading persons suspected of crime
committed in a proclaimed district could be arrested
by a special or provisional warrant, in any part of
Queensland, and be detained in prison; but it was
provided that such persons should be treated as
persons accused of crime and not as convicted
prisoners, and that no person "should be held in
custody under a provisional warrant for a longer
period than thirty days, nor under a special warrant
for a longer period than two months, without being
brought to trial for the offence stated in such warrant." In justification of the measure, the same
Minister quoted cases in which woolsheds had been
burnt and the police and private individuals had
been fired upon although no actual loss of life had
occurred. A stranger cannot form an opinion upon
the question and can only note, on the one side,
that the operation of the Act was limited to one
year, that it was most judiciously administered, not
more than one district, under a single district magistrate, having been proclaimed, and that it brought
about the speedy cessation of the troubles; on the
other, that no attempt was made by the Government
at mediation between the opposing parties, although,
to quote the Attorney-General again, they "knew
that labour troubles of an aggravated nature were
likely to occur." A Bill "to provide for conciliation
in industrial pursuits" is included in the programme
of the Government.

As regards the necessity for humanitarian legislation, reference can be made to the evidence given before a Royal Commission in 1891. The Commissioners were unanimous in reporting that, in many factories and workshops which they had visited, the sanitary conditions were very bad, the ventilation was improperly attended to, and little or no attempt had been made to guard the machinery. They were agreed as to the need of further legislation, but, while some were of opinion that the wider powers should be exercised by inspectors under the local authorities, others were in favour of the appointment of a special class of male and female inspectors. They also found that children of the ages of ten, eleven, and twelve years were employed in factories, and that the hours of labour in many retail shops were very long, adding that medical evidence was conclusive that the excessive hours were more injurious to health in Queensland than they would be in a colder climate ; but they were unable to concur as to the advisability of legislative interference. A Factory Act, though not of a very stringent character, was passed by the Government towards the end of the session of 1896.

The attention of the Government during the last few years has been directed mainly towards the restoration of the credit of the country and the development of its industries. Queensland reached its lowest ebb in 1889, when, in spite of the recent loan of ten millions, the deficit amounted to

£484,000. Since that time matters have rapidly improved, and in 1895 and 1896 the revenue was considerably in excess of the expenditure. This result has been achieved by economical administration, and the direct encouragement of enterprise which has been effected by a large extension of the sphere of State action. The principles involved appear to have been threefold.

First, that the State should facilitate the occupation of outlying districts by the construction of public works, provided they may be expected to return a fair interest upon the expenditure. The proposals put forward some fifteen years ago, that the three Western lines should be connected with the Gulf of Carpentaria by a series of Land Grant Railways, were condemned by the sense of the community, which preferred to postpone their construction until it could be undertaken by the State. In pursuance of this policy all the railways are owned and managed by the State, which has recently protected itself against the danger of the construction of unprofitable lines under political pressure by an Act of Parliament under which, upon any fresh proposal, the local authorities affected may be required to give a guarantee that they will, for a period of years, should the earnings fail to reach a certain standard, make good half of the deficiency out of the rates. In the Western portions of the Colony, in which occupation has been retarded by the scarcity of water, the Government have also

incurred considerable expenditure in the successful
provision of artesian water and in general works
of conservation.

Secondly, that the State may assist producers to
dispose advantageously of their produce. Reference
has been made to the contracts which the Government have entered into with the British India
Company for the carriage of farm and dairy produce.
They are now considering the advisability of assisting
cattle-owners, whose resources are severely strained
by the low prices which they obtain in London for
their frozen meat. The principal cause of the low
prices and the attitude of the Premier can be
gathered from the following extract from the
financial statement which he delivered in 1896 :—

"Our meat I believe to be as good as any in the
world, and the cost at which it can be delivered at
a profit at the ports of the Colony will compare
favourably with any other country that I am aware
of ; and yet the prices lately obtainable in London
are such as barely cover the charges for freezing,
freight, insurance, &c. Something will have to be
done if the industry is to be preserved. The only
suggestion I have received as yet is that the Colony,
either individually or in conjunction with the other
Colonies, should take the business of distribution
into its own hands, as it is believed that, whilst the
consumers give good value for our meat, a great part
of that value is absorbed by various graduations of
middlemen, leaving, as I have said, a margin for the

producer altogether disproportionate to the real value of the product. To effect this a large amount of capital will be required, respecting which I have no proposal to submit, as the matter is really one for private enterprise to undertake, but I mention the matter as one requiring speedy and most serious attention, because, if private enterprise should not be forthcoming to cope with the difficulty, it may devolve upon Parliament to adopt such measures as may appear practicable to conserve an important industry which we can ill afford to lose."

Subsequently, I understand (I was not in Queensland at the time), a Parliamentary Committee was instructed to consider the question, and reported in favour of the establishment at London and in the provinces of depôts for the receipt and distribution of frozen meat.

On another occasion, referring to the injury done to the harbour of Brisbane by excessive towage rates, the Premier said that if private enterprise could not do it for a less sum, it would be a very simple thing for the Government to take the matter in hand.

Thirdly, that the State may use its credit, after strict investigation of the circumstances and upon conviction of the validity of the security, to enable prospective producers to borrow money at a low rate of interest. The Sugar Works Guarantee Act, of which I have quoted the provisions, has led other producers to ask for similar concessions. The farmers want flour mills and cheap money; the pastoralists and graziers complain of the tax levied upon them under the Meat and Dairy Produce Encouragement Acts. Why, they ask, should the sugar industry be exceptionally favoured? Again, if the Government are to establish distributing agencies for frozen meat, why not also for other produce?

The Socialists describe these various measures as a spurious form of socialism calculated to increase the profits of a single class of the community; but the Government do not trouble themselves about abstract terms. They have steadily pursued a settled policy, and have successively assisted the sugar, pastoral, and agricultural interests; they are prepared, if necessary, to give substantial help to cattle-owners in the disposal of their produce, and they intend to propose amendments of the mining laws which will promote the further development of the industry. Nor have the producers alone been benefited; the working classes, who are the first to suffer in times of depression, are sharing in the renewed prosperity of the country, and have been able to take advantage of the increased demand for their services.

IV

THE LAND POLICY OF NEW ZEALAND

Differences of conditions between Australia and New Zealand—
The Public Works policy—Taxation on land—The Land Act
of 1892—The Land for Settlements Acts—The Government
Advances to Settlers Acts—The encouragement of settlement
— The co-operative construction of Public Works — The
unemployed—Continuity of policy.

THE Constitution of 1852, under which New
Zealand obtained responsible government,
differed from those granted to the Australian Provinces in the creation of Provincial as well as
Central Authorities. Owing to the mountainous
character of many parts of both islands, and in
the absence of railways and other facilities for
internal transit, communication had been carried
on principally by sea, and settlement, instead of
radiating from one point, as in New South Wales,
Victoria, and South Australia, had been diffused at
Auckland, Wellington, Christchurch, Dunedin, and
other places of secondary importance. Under
these circumstances, while it was deemed advisable
to create a Central Government at Auckland, which
was transferred to Wellington in 1865, six elective

Provincial Councils were established, which, though their legislative and executive powers were confined within specified limits, promoted the continuance of the separate development of the several portions of the Colony. In 1876 the Provincial Legislatures, which had in the meanwhile been increased by a division of territories to ten, were abolished by the Central Government, principally because they impeded the execution of the national policy of the construction of public works. The effects of the system, however, are still seen, especially in the demands made in the House of Representatives that the different districts shall share in the benefits of any proposed expenditure of public funds.

Another feature which served to differentiate New Zealand from Australia was the existence of a warlike native race in the North Island, which opposed the colonisation of the early settlers. From the outset, ignorance of each other's language and habits of thought led to misunderstandings in regard to the disposal of land, which was complicated by the communal tenure of the Maoris. The appreciation of this difficulty led to the insertion in the Treaty of 1840, in which the chiefs purported to cede the sovereignty of New Zealand, of a provision which reserved to the Crown the right of pre-emption over all native lands. But the dissatisfaction was not allayed ; the natives, conscious of the steady advances of the

settlers and urged to sell by agents of the Crown,
feared that they would gradually be dispossessed of
their territory. A conflict which arose in regard to
some land, and led to fatal results, increased the
state of tension, which culminated, after a struggle
in the extreme north, in the prolonged conflicts of
1860 to 1870. After the pacification the reciprocal
relations began to improve, and are now excellent.
The Maoris are universally respected, have four
members in the House of Representatives, and
two in the Legislative Council, and are represented
in the Executive Council by a Minister, who is
himself a half-caste. Numerous attempts have also
been made to settle the land question, notably by
the resumption of the right of pre-emption, which
had been waived for a time, and by the constitution,
by an Act of 1893, of a Validation Court for the
purpose of considering and finally settling the titles
to lands obtained by Europeans from the natives.
In view of their pre-emptive right, the Government
have been bound, in justice to the Maoris, to
make provision for the purchase of such lands as
may be offered to them, though they have not
herein initiated a new policy. From the establishment of Imperial sovereignty to 1870, successive
Governments acquired six million acres in the
North Island, the whole of the Middle Island,
with the exception of reserves for the original
owners who were few in number, and Stewart
Island. From that date until 1895, another six

million acres had been acquired at an outlay of
a million and a half pounds, and subsequent purchases, from a large area still under negotiation,
amount to about 550,000 acres. New Zealand has
thus disbursed, and is still disbursing, large sums of
money in the purchase of native lands, while
Australia and Tasmania recognised no right of
possession on the part of the few degraded
aboriginals; and New Zealand alone is burdened
with the payment of interest upon loans raised
to cover the charges of prolonged military cam-
paigns.

During the wars, settlement was necessarily
checked in the North Island, but proceeded in
the Middle Island without intermission. At their
conclusion, in 1870, Mr. (now Sir Julius) Vogel,
the Colonial Treasurer, placed before Parliament
a comprehensive scheme of public works, which
aimed at the general improvement of means of
communication, a matter of particular importance
in the North Island as being likely to hasten its
final pacification. "The leading features of the
policy were : to raise a loan of ten millions, and
to spend it over a course of years in systematic
immigration, in the construction of a main trunk
railway throughout the length of each island, in
the employment of immigrants on the railway
work, and in their ultimate settlement within large
blocks of land reserved near the lines of railway, in
the construction of main roads, in the purchase of

native lands in the North Island, in the supply of water-power on the goldfields, and in the extension of the telegraph. The plan, with some modifications, was authorised by the Legislature. These modifications mostly related to the amount to be borrowed and to its expenditure; but there was one alteration which crippled the whole policy. The reservation of large tracts of Crown land through which the railways were intended to be made, with a view to the use of that land for settlement thereon, and as the means of recouping to the Colony a great part of the railway expenditure, was withdrawn by the Government from fear of losing the whole scheme. That fear was not unfounded, inasmuch as provincial opposition to the reservation in question, combined with the opposition of those who disliked the whole scheme, would have seriously endangered its existence." [1] The provincial opposition was due to the fact that, though the disposal of the Crown lands and the appropriation of the Land Fund were vested by the Constitution Act in the Central Legislature, each province had in practice been allowed to frame the regulations for the alienation of land within its district, and had received the proceeds of sale for its own use. But the omission of the proposed reservation " has necessitated the frequent recurrence of borrowing large sums in order to continue work which had been begun and was useless while

---

[1] "The Colony of New Zealand," Gisborne, p. 170.

it was unfinished, instead of making, as would have been the case under a proper system of land reservation, the work itself to a great extent, if not altogether, self-supporting and self-extending; and that deplorable omission has also frustrated the anticipated conduct of progressive colonisation concurrently with the progress of the railways. The result of not insisting on this fundamental condition has been what should have been foreseen and obviated. The Provincial Governments sold land in the vicinity of the intended railways, and expended the proceeds for provincial purposes; and, as a rule, speculative capitalists absorbed the land and the profits which should have been devoted to colonisation and to the railway fund." [1] As the proposed railways would pass through private as well as Crown lands, Sir Julius Vogel also sought the power to levy a special rate, in certain circumstances, upon the persons in the vicinity of the railways who would be benefited by their construction. He believed that he would thereby prevent " indiscriminate scrambling for railways," but was equally unable to induce Parliament to accept his views. The aggregation of large estates was promoted by the low price, 10s. or even 5s. an acre, at which the land was for many years sold. 262 freeholders, including companies, owned in 1891, 7,840,000 acres of land in estates of 10,000 acres and upwards. The Province has, since its

[1] "The Colony of New Zealand," Gisborne, pp. 171-2.

foundation, sold or finally disposed of more than 21 million acres, and has at present nearly three million acres open for selection. The remaining lands, exclusive of those in the hands of the Maoris, amount to 16½ million acres, but comprise large tracts of barren mountainous country in the Middle Island, and of valueless pumice sand in the North Island. In most directions, according to the Premier, settlement is already in advance of the roading operations.

The policy initiated by Sir Julius Vogel in 1870 was carried on by successive Ministers until 1888, during which time more than 27 millions were borrowed and devoted, for the most part, to the construction of railways and other public undertakings. Subsequently, Sir Harry Atkinson and his successor, Mr. John Ballance, realised the danger of constant reliance upon loans, and greatly reduced the expenditure, which had become extravagant in the abundance of borrowed money. Mr. Ballance also reformed the system of direct taxation and gave an impetus to legislation dealing with the settlement of the land and the protection of workmen in industrial pursuits.

The existing property tax, at the rate of one penny in the £ on all property, subject to an exemption of £500, was replaced by a graduated tax on incomes and land values, the principle of graduation having already been recognised in the case of succession duty. The former impost was naturally upheld by

large owners of property and by all classes of professional men who had escaped taxation upon their
incomes ; while it was distasteful to shopkeepers,
who might be taxed on unsaleable merchandise,
and to cultivators of the soil, who found that their
taxes rose in proportion to the improvements which
they effected upon their estates. The Government
had little difficulty in passing their measure, which,
subject to slight modifications, is in force at the
present time. Incomes below £300 are not taxed ;
between £300 and £1,300 they pay 6d. in the £,
above £1,300 a shilling ; but the sum of £300 is
deducted from the total income in the assessment
of the tax. For instance, an income of £2,000 pays
£60, at the rate of £25 upon £1,000, and £35 upon
£700. The ordinary land-tax is a penny in the £
on all freehold properties of which the unimproved
value exceeds £500 ; between £500 and £1,500
exemption is allowed on £500 ; between £1,500
and £2,500 the exemption decreases by £1 for
every £2 of increased value, being extinguished at
the latter amount. Should the value exceed £5,000,
a graduated land-tax is also levied, which rises
progressively from half a farthing, until it reaches
twopence upon estates of the unimproved value of
£210,000 and upwards. All improvements are excluded from the assessment of the taxable amount :
they are defined to include "houses and buildings,
fencing, planting, draining of land, clearing from
timber, scrub or fern, laying down in grass or

pasture, and any other improvement whatsoever, the benefit of which is unexhausted at the time of valuation." Under this provision rural owners have every encouragement to improve their properties, as the more they do so, the smaller becomes the proportion of the total value of their estates on which they are liable for taxation. Owners are allowed, for the purposes of the ordinary, but not of the graduated land-tax, to deduct from the unimproved value of their land the amount of registered mortgages secured upon it ; and mortgagees pay one penny in the £ upon the sum total of their mortgages, but are not subject to the graduated tax. A return, published under the assessment of 1891, shows, however, that rural owners are obtaining less benefit from the exemption of improvements than the owners of urban lands. The figures are as follows :—

	Actual Value, including improvements.	Value of improvements.	Unimproved value.
Counties... ...	85,818,167	27,922,735	57,880,233
Boroughs ...	36,406,862	18,442,562	17,907,662
Total ...	£122,225,029	£46,365,297	£75,787,895

It thus appears that land is taxed, on an average, at 49 per cent. of its actual value inclusive of improvements in boroughs, and at 67½ per cent. in counties ;

but it must be remembered that, as the urban population is not concentrated in one centre, land values
have not been inflated to any great extent, and that
much of the rural land has either recently been
settled or is held in large blocks in a comparatively unimproved condition. The improvement
or sale of such properties would, the Government
believed, be promoted by the imposition of the tax.
The Minister of Labour (the Hon. W. P. Reeves)
expressed this view in the clearest terms: "The
graduated tax is a finger of warning held up to
remind them that the Colony does not want these
large estates. I think that, whether partly or almost
entirely unimproved, they are a social pest, an industrial obstacle, and a bar to progress." Similar
feelings are, apparently, entertained towards the
absentee owner, who, if he has been absent from
or resident out of the Province for at least three years
prior to the passing of the annual Act imposing the
tax, is required to pay an additional 20 per cent.
upon the amount of graduated land-tax to which he
would otherwise be liable. The income and land
taxes produce a revenue about equal to that
formerly derived from the property tax, and are
collected from far fewer taxpayers, the respective
numbers being 15,808 and 26,327 in a population of
some 700,000 persons. The benefits have been
felt principally by tradesmen, miners, mechanics,
labourers, and small farmers. Of 91,500 owners of
land, 76,400 escape payment of the land-tax. It

may be noted, incidentally, that a permissive Act of 1896 authorises such local bodies as adopt it to levy rates on the basis of the unimproved value of land. Much anxiety has been felt by large landowners and owners of urban property throughout Australasia at the successive adoption of a tax on unimproved values by South Australia, New Zealand, and New South Wales. They fear that it is the first step towards the national absorption of land values advocated by Henry George, but forget that the Governments of New South Wales and New Zealand, in respect of exemptions, and of New Zealand and South Australia, in respect of graduation, have introduced features in their systems of taxation which cause them to be fundamentally distinct from his proposals. The Bill passed through the Victorian Assembly in 1894, but rejected by the Council, also provided for exemptions.

But how, it may be asked, has an equitable assessment of the land been secured for the purposes of the tax ? Any owner who is not satisfied with the value placed upon his land on the assessment roll, may require the Commissioner to reduce the assessment to the amount specified on the owner's return, or to purchase the land at the sum mentioned on the owner's return of its actual value inclusive of improvements. The Commissioner is bound to make the reduction unless the Government approve of the acquisition of the land. A reasonable balance is thus struck : the Government are unwilling to have a large amount of land thrown on their hands, while the owner does not take the risk of the resumption of the land at an inadequate valuation. Disputes between the Commissioner and owners have, in most cases, been adjusted satisfactorily; but the Government decided to buy the Cheviot Estate of 85,000 acres, which lies close to the sea in the Middle Island. Upon its purchase they at first let the pastoral lands temporarily at the rate of £8,862 a year, while their surveyors laid out the country and supervised the construction of roads. The results of the transaction were, in 1896, eminently satisfactory; the capital value of the estate then stood at £271,700, and the annual rental at £14,300; and the few inhabitants engaged in pastoral pursuits had been replaced by 216 settlers and their families, who were reported to be of a good class and to have done a large amount of work in the improvement of their lands.

The principal Act dealing with the alienation of Crown Lands is that of 1892, which consolidates and amends former legislation. Crown Lands are divided into urban, suburban, and village lands, which are sold by auction at an upset price, and rural lands, which are again subdivided according to their adaptability for cultivation or pasturage. When townships are being laid out on Crown Lands, one-tenth of the superficial area is to be reserved for purposes of recreation, and a similar extent as a nucleus of municipal property, to be vested subsequently as an endowment in the local authority in addition to the reserves necessary for all public purposes. At the option of the applicant, lands may be purchased for cash, or be selected for occupation with the right of purchase, or on lease in perpetuity. Selectors are limited to 640 acres of first-class land, or 2,000 acres of second-class land, the maximum being inclusive of any lands which they may already hold. The object of this provision is to prevent existing landowners from aggregating large estates by the purchase of Crown Lands. Cash sales are effected at a price of not less than 20s. and 5s. per acre, respectively, for first-class and second-class land, and entitle the selector to a freehold title upon the expenditure of a prescribed amount on improvements. Land selected under occupation with the right of purchase is subject to a rental of 5 per cent. upon the cash price, under lease in perpetuity, which is for 999 years, to a rental of 4 per cent. ; and strict conditions of residence and improvement are, in both cases, attached and rigidly enforced. At the expiration of ten years, a licensee under the former tenure may, upon payment of the upset price, acquire the freehold or may change the license for a lease in perpetuity. The latter is the perpetual lease of the previous Acts, denuded of the option of purchase and of the periodical revaluation of the rent, and is, in the latter respect, reactionary, as the State gives up its right to take advantage of any unearned increment. Subsidies amounting to one-third of the rent of land taken up under any of the above tenures and one-fourth of the rent of small grazing-runs are paid to local authorities for the construction of roads, but must be expended for the benefit of the selectors from whose lands such moneys are derived. The Act of 1892 also authorises the Governor to reserve blocks of country, as special settlements or village settlements, for persons who may desire to take up adjacent lands. The Village Settlements have been successful when they have been formed in localities in which there was a demand for labour ; the Special Settlements comparative failures, because many of the members of the associations had neither the requisite means nor knowledge of rural pursuits. Pastoral land is let by auction in areas capable of carrying not more than 20,000 sheep or 4,000 head of cattle ; or in small grazing-runs not exceeding, according to the quality of the soil, 5,000 or 20,000 acres in area. The dominant feature in the Act, in its application to pastoral as well as agricultural land, is the strict limitation of the area which may be held by any one person ; rightly or wrongly, the Government are determined that the Crown Lands shall not pass into the hands of large holders. The principal transactions of the last three years are thus summarised, the figures for 1894 covering the period from April, 1893, to March, 1894, and so for the other years :

TENURE.	1894.		1895.		1896.	
	No.	AREA.	No.	AREA.	No.	AREA.
		Acres.		Acres.		Acres.
Cash	500	34,999	415	38,710	492	26,584
Occupation, with right to purchase ...	471	108,499	428	75,500	434	84,970
Lease in perpetuity ...	1,228	255,348	1,032	166,037	1,461	199,093
Pastoral runs	227	899,945	123	568,293	188	2,156,378

In regard to the numerical superiority of leases in perpetuity, it must be pointed out that, not only the special blocks, but the improved farms and lands offered under the Land for Settlements Acts, to which I shall have occasion to refer, are disposed of solely under that tenure; but it appears to be attractive in itself : as most of the Crown Lands require considerable outlay before they become productive, a selector can expend any capital that he may possess more advantageously upon the development of the capabilities of the soil than upon the acquisition of the freehold. The Government also are benefited by a policy which renders the land revenue a permanent asset in the finances. The receipts for the financial year 1895–6 amounted to nearly £300,000.

In 1892 an attempt was also made to deal with the problem of the scarcity of available land in settled districts which was caused by the prevalence of large estates. It was thought that the labourers employed upon them, and the sons of farmers who might wish to settle near their parents, should have an opportunity of acquiring land. The Government, accordingly, passed the first of a series of Land for Settlements Acts, which authorised the re-purchase or exchange of lands and their subdivision for purposes of close settlement. Upon the recommendation of a Board of Land Purchase Commissioners, some of whom represent local interests, that a certain estate is suitable for settlement, and should be purchased at a certain price, the Government may enter into negotiations with the owner with a view to a voluntary transaction, and, upon his refusal, take the land compulsorily at a valuation fixed by a Compensation Court. Owners are so far safeguarded that they cannot be dispossessed of estates of less than 640 acres of first-class, or 2,000 acres of second-class land, that they can claim to retain the above area, and that they can require the Government to take the whole of their estates. The maximum annual expenditure was limited at first to £50,000, but has been raised to £250,000. At the end of March of last year twenty-eight estates, containing 87,000 acres, had been acquired, in one case compulsorily, and made available for settlement by surveys and the construction of roads at a total expenditure of nearly £390,000. Nineteen of these had already been subdivided into farms of various sizes, and were bringing in rentals amounting to

4·76 per cent. upon the outlay which they had involved. The Land Purchase Inspector was able to report that the lands, which had been the object of eager competition, had, in most cases, been greatly improved and were in good condition, and he is likely to find even better results in the future, as the Amending Act of 1896 provided that applications for land should not be entertained unless the applicants were able to prove their ability properly to cultivate the soil and to fulfil the stipulations of the leases. This provision is of great importance, as much of the land has been cultivated by its former owners, and would deteriorate rapidly under incapable management. The Governments of South Australia, Queensland, and Western Australia have legislated in a similar direction, and that of New South Wales introduced a Bill which failed to become law. As far as New Zealand is concerned, which has con-ducted its operations on the largest scale, the system has not been sufficiently long in existence to enable an estimate to be formed of its probable financial results.

A similar uncertainty prevails in regard to the more recent attempts to place cheap money within the reach of settlers. The first step in that direction was taken in 1886, when regulations were made for the establishment of Village Settlements, the members of which might receive loans for the construction of their houses and for other purposes. These settlements were not, as in some of the

Australian Provinces, formed on a co-operative or a semi-communistic basis. The success of this experiment doubtless encouraged the Government to widen the scope of the advances. In 1895, 4,560 persons, divided among 144 settlements, had occupied 33,800 acres of land; they had received £25,800 in advances, had paid £17,600 in rent and interest, and had carried out improvements of the value of £92,800. These improvements, consequently, form an ample security for the repayment of the loans. The necessity of a general scheme of advances was based upon the difficulty experienced by small settlers, however good might be the security, in obtaining loans except at prohibitive rates. Authority was, accordingly, obtained through the Government Advances to Settlers Acts of 1894–6 to borrow three millions with a view to loans ranging from £25 to £3,000, upon first mortgages, to owners of freehold land and occupiers of Crown Lands, the advances not to exceed three-fifths of the value of the former and one-half of the value of the lessee's interest in the latter. Advances may not be made on town lands, nor on suburban lands which are held for residential or manufacturing purposes. The valuation of every security is to be carried out by or on behalf of a superintendent appointed *ad hoc.*, and is to be submitted for the consideration of a General Board consisting of the Colonial Treasurer, the Superintendent, the Public Trustee, the Commissioner of Taxes, and a nominee of the

Governor in Council. The advances on freehold
land may be either for a fixed period at 5 per cent.,
or for 36½ years at 6 per cent., of which 5 per cent.
is reckoned as interest and 1 per cent. towards the
gradual repayment of the principal ; on leasehold
lands, in the latter form alone. As the loan of a
million and a half raised as the source of advances
was floated at 3 per cent., and realised nearly
£1,400,000, the margin between the percentage due
by the Government and that received from the
settlers should be sufficient to enable one-tenth of
the interest to be paid, as provided, into an Assurance Fund against possible losses, and a residue to
be available which will cover the general expenses
of administration. But it is obvious that the result
of the experiment will depend greatly upon the
prevalent rate of interest and the price of produce.
Hitherto, two-thirds of the advances have been used
by settlers to enable them to rid themselves of
former and less advantageous mortgages ; in some
cases, mortgagees, in order to retain their mortgages, have voluntarily lowered the rate of interest
to 5 per cent. The tabular statement on the
following page of the financial position is the
latest that has been issued, and does not pur-
port to be more than approximately correct. Advances may also be made towards the construction
of dwelling-houses to those who have obtained
selections under the Land for Settlements Acts ;
but they may not exceed twenty pounds nor the

amount already spent by the applicant upon his holding.

INCOME.

The advances authorised and accepted amount to £735,967, and yield an annual income of 5 per cent.	£36,798
The temporary investment of £603,444 in Government securities yields an annual income at the rate of 3·42 per cent. ...	20,747
The balance of £51,805 on current account with the Bank, may be estimated to yield 2 per cent.	1,036
Estimated total income on June 15, 1896 ...	£58,581

EXPENDITURE.

Annual charge for interest at 3 per cent. on £1,500,000	£43,000
Salaries for the year	3,700
Other expenses	2,800
Mortgage Tax, estimated	1,800
Estimated total expenditure...	£53,300
Balance of income over expenditure ...	5,281
	£58,581

Another measure which may affect the well-being of settlers is the Family Home Protection Act, 1895. Any owner of land may settle as a family home the land, not exceeding, with all improvements, £1,500 in value, on which he resides and has his home, provided that at the time the land is unencumbered and he is able to pay all his debts without the land in question. As a precaution against the conceal-

ment of liabilities, he is obliged to make an application to a District Land Registrar, who must
thereupon give public notice of the intended registration. Should any creditor put in a claim within
twelve months, the case is to be tried before a Judge
of the Supreme Court, and if the owner of the land is
vindicated, the Registrar is to issue a certificate which
will exempt the family home from seizure under
ordinary processes of law, but not in one or two
contingencies, of which the principal is the failure
to meet current liabilities in respect of rates or taxes.
The registration is to continue until the death of
the owner or the majority or death under the age of
twenty-one of all his children, and is not to precede
the last of these events. Upon its cessation it may
be renewed at the option of the persons then holding
the estate, who must be relations of the deceased.
Little effect has been given to the Act owing,
probably, to the unavoidable publicity of the proceedings. It appears to have been based upon a
South Australian Act of 1891, which enables holders
of workmen's blocks, by the endorsement of their
leases, to secure for their properties somewhat
similar exemptions from seizure. Their failure to
avail themselves, to any considerable extent, of this
privilege is attributed to the unwillingness of
working men to take any trouble in a matter of
which the advantages are merely contingent.

So far I have discussed the legislation of New
Zealand which affects freeholders and those who

are, or desire to become, tenants of the Crown ; but
before proceeding to deal with matters of common
import to most settlers, I must point out that tenants
holding from private landlords have also engaged
the paternal attention of the Government. The
Minister of Lands introduced last session, but failed
to pass, a Fair Rent Bill, which would have established a system of Land Courts under the presidency
of Stipendiary Magistrates. Landlords and tenants
would have had an equal right to apply for the
determination of the fair rent which, upon the
decision of the Court, whether it were higher or
lower than the reserved rent, would have been
deemed, until a further revision, to be the rent
payable under the lease. The Government displayed great inconsistency in the introduction of the
measure ; having shown, in the system of lease in
perpetuity, that they objected to the periodical
revaluation of the rents payable upon Crown Lands,
they proposed, through the Fair Rent Bill, to enable
the Crown, as landlord, to take steps to increase the
rents of its tenants.

As regards the general interests of producers, the
Government have, through reductions amounting to
£50,000 a year in railway rates, made a concession
to them at the expense of the general taxpayer, as
the railways, after payment of working expenses,
return only 2·8 per cent., a sum insufficient to meet
the interest upon their cost of construction. Again,
they have appointed experts in butter-making, fruit-

growing, &c., who travel about the country and give
technical instruction by means of lectures ; and
they distribute, among farmers and others, pamphlets containing practical advice upon various aspects
of cultivation. But, except that butter is received,
graded and frozen free of charge, they have not
followed the example of Victoria and South Australia in the direct encouragement of exports.
Finally, while the State acts as landlord, banker,
and carrier, it also carries on a department of life
insurance and annuities, accepts the position of
trustee under wills, and, if the programme of the
Government is accepted by Parliament, will undertake the business of fire insurance and grant a small
allowance to all who are aged and indigent and
have resided for a long term of years in the Colony.

The development of the resources of the country,
under the assistance of the State, has also proceeded
in other directions. More than £500,000 had been
spent up to March, 1896, in the construction
of water-races on goldfields for the benefit of
alluvial miners and public companies ; and in that
year the Premier, in view of the large amount of
foreign and native capital that was flowing into the
industry, obtained the authorisation of Parliament
to the expenditure of a further sum of £200,000 in
the conservation of water by means of large reservoirs, the construction of water-races, the extension
of prospecting throughout the Colony, and the
construction of roads and tracks for the general

development of the goldfields. The physical attractions and health resorts of the country, many of which are reached with difficulty, are also being opened up by the expenditure of public funds.

The general question of settlement has, during the last few years, been connected closely with that of the unemployed. In New Zealand, as in several of the Australian Provinces, the construction of the main lines of railway attracted into the country immigrants who, upon their completion, were left without other resources. At the same time the fall in prices rendered many settlers unable to fulfil their obligations, and, upon the loss of their properties, drove them into the towns, where they swelled the ranks of the unemployed. It also forced those who remained solvent to cut down their general expenses, and especially their labour bill, to the lowest possible point. The Government were compelled to face the problem and attempted to give former settlers a fresh chance and gradually to accustom artisans to rural pursuits which, in the case of uncleared land, are at first of a simple character. But the facilities offered under the Land Act were of little use unless it could be arranged that the men, being without capital, should have outside employment upon which they could depend until their lands had been cleared and brought into cultivation. It had already been realised that the construction of roads was an indispensable sequel to that of railways, and large annual appropriations had been made from the Public Works Fund ; but it was then decided that settlement should be encouraged systematically in those districts in which it was proposed to proceed with the construction of roads. This policy has, accordingly, been carried out energetically during the last few years from loans and current revenue upon the co-operative system, which was inaugurated in 1891 by the Hon. R. J. Seddon, then Minister of Public Works and now Premier of the Colony. As this system, which was first tried as an experiment upon the railways, is now employed in connection with most public works, its object and operation may be illustrated by a series of quotations : " The contract system had many disadvantages. It gave rise to a class of middle men, in the shape of contractors, who often made large profits out of their undertakings, and at times behaved with less liberality to their workmen than might have been expected under the circumstances. Even in New Zealand, where the labour problem is less acute than in older countries, strikes have occurred in connection with public works contracts, with the result that valuable time has been lost in the prosecution of the works, much capital has been wasted by works being kept at a standstill and valuable plant lying idle, and large numbers of men being for some time unemployed ; and considerable bitterness of feeling has often been engendered. The contract system also gave rise to sub-contracting, which is worse again ; for not only

is it subject to all the drawbacks of the parent
system, but by relegating the conduct of the works
to contractors of inferior standing, with little or no
capital, the evil of "sweating" was admitted. Very
often, too, the business people who supplied stores
and materials were unable to obtain payment for
them, and not seldom the workmen also failed to
receive the full amount of their wages. The result
in some cases was that, instead of the expenditure
proving a great boon to the district in which the
works were situated, as would have been the case if
the contract had been well managed and properly
carried out, such contracts frequently brought
disaster in their train. The anomaly of the principal contractor making a large profit, his sub-
contractor being ruined and his workmen left
unpaid, also occasionally presented itself, and thus
the taxpayer who provided the money had the
mortification of seeing one man made rich (who
would perhaps take his riches to Europe or America
to enjoy them) and a number of others reduced to
poverty, or in some instances cast upon public
charity. . . . The co-operative system was designed
to overcome these evils, and to enable the work to
be let direct to the workmen, so that they should be
able, not only to earn a fair day's wage for a fair
day's work, but also to secure for themselves the
profits which a contractor would have otherwise
made on the undertaking. . . . The work is valued
by the engineer appointed to have charge of it

before it is commenced, and his valuations are
submitted to the Engineer-in-Chief of the Colony
for approval. When approved, they constitute the
contract price for the work ; but they are not
absolutely unchangeable as in the case of a binding, strictly legal contract. It frequently happens
under an ordinary contract that work turns out to
be more easy of execution than was anticipated, and
the State has to see its contractors making in-
ordinate profits. Sometimes, on the other hand,
works cost more than was expected ; but in most
cases of this kind the contractor either becomes a
bankrupt, so that the State has, after all, to pay full
value for the work, or, if the contractor happens to
be a moneyed man, he will probably find some
means of getting relieved of a contract, or of
obtaining special consideration for his losses on
completion of his work. Under the co-operative
system, if it is found that the workmen are earning
unusually high rates their contracts can be determined, and be re-let at lower rates, either to the
same party of men or to others, as may be
necessary. Similarly, if it is shown, after a fair
trial of any work, that capable workmen are not
able to earn reasonable rates upon it, the prices
paid can, with the approval of the Engineer-in-
Chief, be increased, so long as the department is
satisfied that the work is not costing more than it
would have cost if let by contract at ordinary fair
paying prices. . . . Another great advantage of co-

operation is that it gives the Government complete control over its expenditure. Under the old plan, when large contracts were entered into, the expenditure thereunder was bound to go on, even though, through sudden depression or other unlooked-for shrinking of the revenue, the Government would gladly have avoided or postponed the outlay. . . . Not only has the Government complete control over the expenditure, but in the matter of the time within which works are to be completed the control is much superior to that possessed when the works are in the hands of a contractor. When once a given time is allowed to a contractor in which to complete a work, any request to finish it in less time would at once provoke a demand for extra payment; but under the co-operative system the Government reserves the right to increase the numbers employed in any party to any extent considered desirable, so that if any sudden emergency arises, or an unusually rapid development in any district takes place, it is quite easy to arrange for the maximum number possible of men being employed on the works in hand, with no more loss of time than is required to get the men together." [1]

It was at first proposed that the men should work in gangs of about fifty, who should have an equal interest in the contract and make an equal division of the wages and profits; but experience showed that large gangs did not work together harmoniously

[1] New Zealand Official Year Book, 1894. Report by Under-Secretary of Public Works.

owing to differences, not only in the temperament
of the men, but also in their abilities as workmen.
The labourers solved this difficulty by forming
themselves into small parties composed of men of
about equal ability, with the result that, while some
gangs earn higher wages than others, the weak are
r.ot excluded altogether from employment. The
co-operative works have, on the whole, been successful; but it is clear, from the reports of the
surveyors, that constant supervision is necessary,
and that there is considerable dissatisfaction, among
unskilled workmen, with the low rate of their earnings, and, generally, with the intermittent character
of the employment. For the Government have
decided, in order that work may be given to as
many as possible and that settlement may be promoted, that no labourers shall be employed more
than four days in the week. During the remainder
of the time, if they have taken up land in the
neighbourhood, they devote themselves to it;
otherwise they are likely to be demoralised by
enforced idleness. The Minister of Public Works
attempted to prove that works had been carried out
more economically under the co-operative system,
but was unable to cite cases that were exactly
analogous. He showed that the average number
of employés had risen from 788 in 1891–2 to 2,336
in 1895–6, but that, whereas in the former years
workmen under the Public Works Department were
twice as numerous as those under the Lands

Department, in the latter the proportion had been more than reversed. This change must be regarded as satisfactory, as employés under the Lands Department are, in a large majority of cases, settlers.

In 1894 the Government passed an Act which was intended to meet the special requirements of the unemployed. Any number of men composing an association may, by agreement with the Minister of Lands, settle upon Crown Lands for the purpose of clearing or otherwise improving them, and will, subject to the authorisation of Parliament, receive from the Colonial Treasurer payment for their work. They are entitled thereupon to take up holdings at a rental based on the combined value of the land in an unimproved condition and of the improvements. This system, which is known as that of Improved Farm Settlements, has been worked largely in connection with co-operative works. In March of last year 39 settlements had been initiated which covered 63,600 acres and carried 679 residents. They have " had the effect of removing from the towns a considerable number of people who otherwise would have been found in the ranks of the unemployed, and an opportunity has been given to all who are really desirous of becoming *bonâ-fide* settlers to make homes for themselves, and become producers rather than a burden on the State. Many who have taken up land on this system brought no experience with

them to aid in the operations of the pioneer work
of settlement, and this had to be gained at some
cost to themselves and the State. So long as the
Government continues monetary aid by way of
assisting in clearing, grassing, and house-building,
all will go well; by the time this comes to an end,
sufficient experience should have been gained, and
the farms ought to be stocked. This latter is at
present a difficulty with many of the settlers, for
it is obvious that many of them can at first do
little more than support themselves out of the
moneys advanced for clearing, without sparing anything for stock." [1] The success of these settlements,
it is pointed out, depends upon the simultaneous
occupation by men with capital of the adjoining
Crown Lands in larger holdings on which there will
be a demand for the labour of the settlers; otherwise they will be in difficulties when the roads are
completed, as their blocks of a hundred acres or
so will not alone suffice to secure to them a livelihood. This principle has been borne in view, as far
as possible, in the location of the settlements.

Labourers for the co-operative works, I should
have stated, are recommended by the local agencies
of the Labour Department, and are selected on the
principle that applicants not previously employed
have priority of claim over those who have recently
had employment; that men resident in the neighbourhood of the works have priority over non-

[1] Report of Department of Lands and Survey, 1896; page iv.

residents, and that married men have priority over single men ; while the qualifications of the men as workmen and their personal characters are naturally taken into consideration. During the five years of its existence, the Labour Department has found employment for nearly 16,000 men ; of the 2,781 men assisted during the year ending March, 1896, 2,163 were sent to Government works. Under the control of the Labour Department is a State Farm, in the province of Wellington, at which unemployed are received for a few weeks or months, and, having saved a few pounds, are enabled to seek work elsewhere. The farm is specially adapted for young, able-bodied men who have been brought up as clerks and shop assistants, but, owing to the stress of competition, have been thrown out of employment. Many of them would be prepared to undertake manual labour, but lack the necessary experience. At the farm they would be able to obtain in a short time sufficient knowledge to render them capable of accepting work for private employment. The Secretary of the Department of Labour, Mr. Tregear, maintains that the farm has proved its usefulness and should be supplemented by similar institutions in the other provinces. Since the last annual report, I understand, the Government have decided, as the land has been improved to a point which renders it impossible to employ any considerable number upon it profitably, to dispose of it, and to remove the workmen

9

to fresh areas of uncleared land. They hope to
recoup themselves for their whole expenditure,
but will not necessarily be convicted of failure
should they fail to do so, as the undertaking was
started on a charitable, and not on a commercial,
basis. It aimed at the assistance of the genuine unemployed, and was not intended to become a refuge
for confirmed loafers. On this point Mr. Tregear
writes, and his views are those of the working
men of New Zealand : " I am more and more impressed with the necessity that exists of establishing
farms which shall be used as places of restriction
for the incurably vagrant atoms of the population.
The State Farm does not and should not fulfil this
purpose ; it is for the disposal and help of worthy
persons, unsuccessful for the time, or failing through
advance in years. What is required is a place of
detention and discipline. There exists in every
town a certain number of men whose position
vibrates between that of the loafer and the criminal :
these should altogether be removed from cities.
The spieler, the bookmaker, the habitual drunkard,
the loafer on his wife's earnings, the man who has
no honest occupation, he whose condition of
'unemployed' has become chronic and insoluble
—all these persons are evil examples and possible
dangers. Such an one should be liable, on conviction before a stipendiary magistrate, to be
removed for one or two years to a farm, where
simple food and clothes would be found for him

in return for his enforced labour. The surroundings would be more healthy, and open-air life and regular occupation would induce more wholesome habits and principles than the hours formerly spent in the beer-shop and at the street-corner, while the removal from bad companionship would liberate from the pressure of old associations. He would, on his discharge, probably value more highly his liberty to work as a free man for the future, and, as the State would have been to no cost for his maintenance, it would be a gainer by his temporary removal from crowded centres. There need be no more trouble than before in regard to the sustentation of the restricted person's family, as such a vagrant is of no use to his family, but only an added burden. While for the honest workman, temporarily 'unemployed,' every sympathy should be shown and assistance to work given, for the other class, the 'unemployable,' there should be compulsory labour, even if under regulations of severity such as obtain in prisons." [1] New Zealand has a justification for penal colonies lacking in older countries in the fact that the genuine unemployed can obtain assistance from the Government to enable them to settle on the land, either through the Co-operative Works or the Improved Farm Settlements.

The special efforts of the Government to settle impecunious persons on the land are still in the

[1] Report of Department of Labour, 1896; page vii.

initial stage and have not served to neutralise the
effects of the lowness of prices and consequent
scarcity of employment.   The total expenditure
under the heading of Charitable Aid was £106,500
in the year ended March, 1896, being an increase of
£20,000 upon that of the previous twelve months.
A sum of £18,000 was also spent on relief works.
The administration is vested in the local authorities,
who obtain the necessary funds from rates, voluntary
contributions and subsidies on a fixed scale from
the National Exchequer.   They expend one-fifth of
the amount on the maintenance of destitute children
and the greater portion of the remainder on out-
door relief.   No information is available as to the
number of persons relieved, their average ages,
the form of relief or the conditions under which
it is given ; but it is evident from reports of the
Inspector of Charitable Institutions that the administration is exceedingly lax and tends to intensify the evil which it should strive to alleviate.
It would seem that, on the one hand, the Government are inculcating habits of independence,
on the other, conniving at the encouragement of
pauperism.

The results of recent legislation will depend,
partly, on the price of produce, principally, on
the methods of administration.   This matter is
one on which it is difficult to form an adequate
opinion, as all statements are tinged more or less
with the prejudice of partisanship.   It is therefore

best to confine oneself to Acts of Parliament and
official documents while realising that the more a
State extends its sphere of action, the more are its
Ministers subject to political pressure and tempted
to maintain themselves in office by a misuse of the
possibilities of patronage. The disposal of Crown
Lands is vested in Local Land Boards, which consist of the Commissioners of Crown Lands for the
district, and of not less than two nor more than four
members appointed for two years, but removable
from time to time by warrant under the hand of the
Governor. These Boards receive all applications
for Crown Lands and dispose of them in accordance with the provisions of the Land Acts. They
are constituted the sole judges of the fulfilment of
the conditions attached to leases and may cancel
them, after inquiry, subject to the right of appeal
to a judge of the Supreme Court. If any lessee
make default in the payment of interest, his lease
is liable to absolute forfeiture, subject to a similar
right of appeal, without any compensation for his
improvements. This question is one of great
delicacy : it is manifestly unfair to confiscate a
man's improvements if he has a fair prospect of
being able to meet his obligations within a definite
period ; on the other hand, if such latitude be
allowed, possibilities of favouritism are at once
admitted. Again, are all applicants for land to
be treated alike, irrespective of the probability
that they will be good tenants of the Crown ? The

Land Boards are vested with a discretionary power to refuse applications, but must state the grounds of their refusal. The best constitution for these Boards has been much discussed; but if, as has been proposed, nomination by the local authorities or election by the electors of local authorities were substituted for nomination of the Government, the pressure might be not only greater, but more immediate. Statistics, moreover, show that the administration of the Land Laws has not erred on the side of leniency. In March, 1896, the arrears of rent throughout the Province were only £15,700, a decrease of £22,000 upon the amount reported for the previous twelve months; and forfeitures had been numerous for failure to carry out the conditions of tenure. Under exceptional circumstances Parliament is prepared to make special arrangements. In view of the losses incurred by pastoralists during the severe winter of 1895, it passed a Pastoral Tenants' Relief Act, which empowered the Land Boards after inquiry into the facts of each case to grant remissions of rent or extensions of leases at reduced rentals. The Advances to Settlers Act also appears to be administered prudently, on the principle that the value of the property which may be offered as a security for a loan, and the risk of any loss from granting an advance, must determine the result of the consideration of every application. It is a necessary limitation of the Act that many of those who most require assistance, having borrowed at high rates of interest, are unable to obtain the advances which would enable them to clear off their mortgages on account of the depreciation in value of the security. Of 2,196 applications received to March of last year, 730 had been refused, and 397 had lapsed through the refusal of the department to offer amounts equal to the expectations of the applicant.

The Acts providing for the purchase of private and native land and for advances to settlers have necessitated a large increase in the indebtedness of the Colony, and a consequent divergence from the principles laid down by Sir Harry Atkinson and Mr. Ballance. The present Premier, Mr. Seddon, who succeeded Mr. Ballance in 1893, admits that his Government borrowed £3,800,000 in three years, but contends that the whole of the amount with the exception of £210,000 is being expended in such a manner as to be remunerative. The sum mentioned is exclusive of a loan for a million authorised last session, which is to be expended upon the construction of railways and roads, the purchase of native lands, and the development of the goldfields and hot springs. Have these loans been in the best interests of the Colony? A stranger can but look at the matter broadly and will be inclined to think that they follow, in natural sequence, upon the policy of Sir Julius Vogel. The State then decided that it would use its credit to accelerate the construction of railways and roads and open up outlying districts. Such works were valueless—in fact ruinous to the Province—unless they were followed by a strenuous and successful encouragement of settlement and cultivation. The latter task has been the principal work of the Seddon Government, which has attempted, not only to settle people on the land, but to settle them in suitable localities and under conditions that will give them a reasonable prospect of an independent and comfortable livelihood.

V

CHARACTERISTICS OF VICTORIAN LEGISLATION

Comparisons between the Australasian Upper Houses—Conflicts between the two Houses in Victoria—The proposed obviation of deadlocks—The utility of the Legislative Council—The antagonism between Town and Country—The Factory Acts, their justification and provisions—State Socialism : Railways, Irrigation Works, the encouragement of Mining, Subsidies and Bonuses, State advances to Settlers—The Unemployed and the Leongatha Labour Colony.

THE Victorian Legislative Council is, from the democratic point of view, the most objectionable of all the Australasian Upper Houses. In Queensland, New South Wales, and New Zealand, the members of the Council are nominated for life and receive no remuneration for their services ; but, as their number is not restricted, their opposition to measures passed by the Assembly is limited by the dread that the Executive may exercise the power of making additional appointments. In the other Provinces the Councils are elective ; in South Australia, Western Australia, and Tasmania, as in the Provinces already mentioned, the Members are subject to no property qualification, and in New Zealand, South Australia, and Tasmania they are paid at the rate, respectively, of £150, £200, and £50 a year. In Victoria, on the other hand, there is a property qualification for membership which consists in the possession of a freehold estate of the clear annual value of £100, which confines eligibility to a small fraction of the population ; and the area of selection is restricted further by the absence of remuneration and by the size of the electoral districts, which necessitates heavy expenditure on the part of a candidate at a contested election. Under these circumstances, the comparatively low electoral franchise, which admits upon the rolls two-thirds of the voters for members of the Assembly, is absolutely useless to the democratic electors : they are unable to find candidates who will adopt their views, and have been obliged, as at the last elections, to allow all the retiring members to be re-elected without opposition. It should be stated that the members are elected for a period of six years in ten provinces, and retire in rotation at intervals of two years.

The Victorian Assembly consists of ninety-five members who are elected for three years upon the basis of manhood suffrage and receive remuneration at the rate of £270 a year. Conflicts between the two Houses were incessant during the first twenty-five years of Responsible Government. Immediately after its establishment in 1855 a struggle arose as to the right of selection upon pastoral properties, in which the Council supported the interests of the squatters. The issue could not be doubtful, as the squatters, who had been allowed to depasture enormous tracts of land in the early days of the Province, had no fixed tenure and were impeding the settlement of the country. In 1865 the Assembly passed a protective tariff which was distasteful to the Council as representative of the producers, and tried to secure its enactment by tacking it on to the Appropriation Bill. They relied upon the section of the Constitution Act which provides that "all Bills for appropriating any part of the revenue of Victoria, and for imposing any duty, rate, tax, rent, return or impost, shall originate in the Assembly, and may be rejected but not altered by the Council." Upon the refusal of the Council to submit to such coercion, the Ministry arranged with various banks that they should advance the funds required for public purposes, levied a tax upon a resolution of the Assembly and paid the civil servants without parliamentary authority. A general election followed, at which the Ministry were successful; the Assembly and Council repeated their action of the previous session, and, finally, the Council agreed to accept the new tariff provided it was submitted to them in the form of a separate Bill. Similar constitutional struggles occurred in 1867 upon the proposed grant to ex-Governor Darling, and in 1877 upon the Bill to provide for the payment of Members of the Assembly. During the following years peace reigned between the two Houses, owing at first to the great prosperity of the Province, which caused universal confidence, and the predominance of material considerations; afterwards to the equally great reaction which compelled politicians to sink their differences and combine to save the credit of their country.

The antagonism was renewed in 1894 upon the proposals for additional taxation, by which the Premier, Mr. Turner, hoped to cope with an anticipated deficiency in the revenue of more than half a million pounds. His scheme included the repeal of the existing land-tax, under which landed estates of upwards of 640 acres in extent are taxed annually upon the excess of the capital value over £2,500— an impost which obviously penalises rural, at the expense of urban, properties and was intended to promote the subdivision of the land (though it does not appear to have had much effect in that direction) ; and the imposition of a tax on unimproved values at the rate of 1d. in the £, subject to the exemption of £100 when the value does not exceed £1,000, and of an income tax which, subject to the exemption of incomes not exceeding £200, was to be at the rate of 3d. in the £ on incomes derived from personal exertion and 6d. on incomes derived from property up to £2,200, above which sum the amount was in both cases to be doubled. Absentees were to pay an additional 20 per cent.,

and incomes from land were to be exempt where
the owner paid the land-tax. These taxes, it was calculated, would yield an annual revenue of £600,000.
The Finance Bill was passed in the Assembly at
its second reading by a majority of twenty-two,
but in committee it was amended so as to exempt
from the land-tax land values of less than £500.
The resultant deficiency in the proceeds of the tax
was made up by a continuance of the primage duties
and by an increase of the tax on incomes derived
from personal exertion. Upon its transmission to
the Council the Bill was summarily rejected, the
Minister who was in charge of it alone, beyond the
tellers, being in its favour, on the ground that the
questions of a tax on unimproved values had not
been submitted to the electorate and that, in the
existing conditions of the Province, any further
burden upon the producers would be opposed to
its best interests. The Ministry accepted the decision
of the Council and contented themselves with rigid
retrenchment, the continuance of the existing land-
tax, and the imposition of a progressive income tax
which rises to a maximum of sixteen-pence upon
the excess over £2,000 of incomes derived from
property. According to a statement of the Premier,
they intend to make the question a distinct issue at
the next elections, and will in the meanwhile take
no action in the matter.

In the following session the Council rejected an
Electoral Bill which provided for the abolition of

the plural vote and the enfranchisement of women, and disagreed with the Assembly upon several important clauses of a Factory Bill, in the legitimate exercise of the functions of a revising Chamber. The Ministry succeeded in 1896 in passing the Factory Bill in a form which met some of the objections of the Council, and reintroduced the Electoral Bill, which was subsequently laid aside by the Council on the ground that it had not secured in the Assembly the absolute majority of all the votes required in the case of amendments to the Constitution.

The value of any Second Chamber must rest upon its ability, and the exercise of its ability, to check dangerous tendencies in legislation. As regards Victoria, it must be admitted that the greatest danger has lain in the tendency to extravagant expenditure due to the fatal facility of obtaining almost unlimited advances from the British capitalist. Politicians have been tempted to outbid each other in the struggle for popular support, and to promise the outlay of vast sums of borrowed money. Judged with reference to this question, the Legislative Council cannot be regarded as having been efficient. The greatest waste of money has occurred in connection with the construction of railways from which there was no likelihood of adequate returns, and with injudicious advances to Irrigation and Water Supply Trusts. The Council has been hampered by the restrictions imposed upon it by the Constitution Act, but it has not admitted that it is debarred from amending Railway Bills, though it has done so but sparingly, owing to the opposition which such action aroused in the Assembly. It would seem that, at the time of the greatest output of the Victorian gold mines and of the high prices obtainable for agricultural and pastoral produce, the Council was as much carried away by the prosperity of the Province as the Assembly, and formed an equally false estimate as to its continuance. It appears, however, to have been the first to realise the imminence of a reaction. A comparison of the British and Victorian finances shows that while, in the former case, speaking broadly, provision is made only for the maintenance of the public services and for some matters of national importance, such as public instruction, in which all parts of the country share equally, in the latter case the expenditure includes the construction of public works which benefit particular localities, and grants and subsidies which benefit particular industries. Under these conditions members of the Assembly are subject to continual pressure from their constituents, which, it is contended, the members of the Council, owing to the greater size of the constituencies, are better able to resist. As the whole body of the taxpayers are responsible for the interest on the railways, a locality has everything to gain by the increase of its mileage ; if it receives advances for works of irrigation and defaults upon the consequent obligations, it hopes to induce the Government, through its Member, to grant more lenient terms. The works in many cases are of doubtful value; the liability remains as a burden upon posterity.

The evil is widely recognised, but opinions differ as to the remedy. A step in the right direction was taken by the appointment in 1890 of the Parliamentary Standing Committee on Railways, which, it is suggested, should be supplemented by a similar Committee whose duty it would be to report upon all proposals for new works of water supply involving an expenditure of a thousand pounds of State money. Others ask that the Council should be allowed to amend Money Bills, and would do so with more reason if the property qualification for membership were removed, as the electorate already includes the bulk of the stable elements of the population. But the greatest safeguard would appear to lie in the lessons of the past, and in the appointment of Standing Committees whose antecedent sanction shall be essential to proposals for the expenditure of national funds upon public undertakings. It would be advisable to define by Act of Parliament what classes of public works might be carried out upon borrowed money ; all others would then form a charge upon current revenue.

The absence of any ultimate appeal in the case of a divergence of opinion between the two Houses has recently been discussed in several of the Provinces. It has been pointed out that the power of the Executive to make additional appointments to nominee Councils is an unsatisfactory device calculated to produce friction between the Governor and his responsible advisers ; that elective Councils can force upon the Assembly dissolutions from which they are themselves exempt ; and that, in the majority of cases, the Councils are able, owing to the variety of issues and the influence of local and personal considerations, to deny that any particular question has received the verdict of popular approval. The measures rejected by the Victorian Council since 1891 include the Land and Income Tax Bill, the Opium Bill, the Miners' Right Titles Bill, the Mallee Land Bill, and the Village Settlements Amendment Bill. The Council has rejected the Opium Bill twice, and the Bill for the abolition of plural voting three times.

The question was considered in 1894 by a Victorian Royal Commission, which recommended that :—

"(1) If the Legislative Assembly shall in two con-secutive sessions pass any Bill which shall not be passed by the Legislative Council, then, notwith-standing such Bill when passed in the second session by the Legislative Assembly shall be in an amended form, if the same shall not in such second session be passed by the Legislative

Council, such Bill, if the Assembly so determine by resolution, shall, in manner to be duly provided, be submitted for acceptance or rejection to the voters on the roll for the Legislative Assembly.

"(2) In the event of the said Bill being duly accepted or approved of by the majority of the voters on the said roll who shall vote when a poll is taken, and upon a certificate to that effect to be duly given by the Speaker, the said Bill shall be transmitted to the Governor for his assent. Should, however, such Bill be rejected or disapproved of, then, upon the certificate of the Speaker to that effect, the said Bill shall lapse for the session.

"(3) At least six weeks must intervene between the first and the second passing of the said Bill by the Legislative Assembly."

Measures based upon these lines were introduced during 1896 in the Assemblies of Victoria, Tasmania, and New South Wales, but, in the latter case alone, reached the Legislative Council. It was thought that that body might receive the Bill favourably, as it would be brought thereby into direct contact with the people, and might overcome the jealousy which is at present felt against it. In fact, it might attain to actual popularity by enabling the electorate to pronounce directly upon a distinct issue. But this view did not prevail with the Council, which rejected the measure in the most summary manner.

A supplementary proposal put forward in Victoria

is that, upon subjects which cannot be referred in a clear and simple manner to the electors, differences should be followed by a dissolution of both Houses, and, if an agreement is still impossible, by their joint meeting as one Chamber. In New Zealand, a Bill recently introduced by the Premier, but not passed through the House of Representatives, provided that, if a measure had been twice within fourteen months passed by one House and rejected by the other, the House which had passed it might call upon the Governor to convene a joint meeting of the two Houses, which should finally dispose of it by approval, rejection, or amendment. It will be noticed that the Council might thus secure the enactment of a measure which was opposed by the majority of the popular representatives.

The antagonism of the two Houses in Victoria would seem to be to a great extent a reflex of an antagonism between town and country. The population of the Province is estimated to have been 1,180,000 in 1895, that of Melbourne and its suburbs 439,000, or 37 per cent. of the whole. Under these conditions, and owing to the greater cohesion of compact electorates, a strong feeling has arisen in the rural districts that Melbourne has a disproportionate voice in the affairs of the Province, and that the balance should be redressed by the action of the Council. It is also believed that the abolition of the plural vote would lead to equal electoral districts which would increase the supremacy of the capital and the power of the Labour Party. At the present time they hold fifteen seats, all of which are urban or suburban, and, though discredited by the collapse of the Trades Unions, are not without influence upon the Government.

The percentage of the total population contained in Melbourne and its suburbs rose from 26 in 1861 to 43 in 1891, mainly as the result of the high protective tariff which aimed at making Victoria the principal manufacturing centre of Australia. Upon the consequent establishment of a large number of factories, the Government were soon compelled to intervene in the interests of the workers, and passed in 1873 the first Act dealing with the supervision of factories and workrooms. It defined a factory as any place in which not less than ten persons were employed in manufacturing goods for sale, and provided that such places should be subject, as to building, sanitation, &c., to regulations made by the central Board of Health, and that no female should be employed therein without the permission of the Chief Secretary for more than eight hours in any one day. The measure failed in its purpose through the indifference of the Municipalities, which were charged with its entire administration. They appear to have been negligent in exercising the powers entrusted to them, and to have allowed themselves to be served by officers who were unacquainted with their duties. In the following years several measures were passed which

were consolidated by the Factories and Shops Act
of 1890. Some new points of great importance had
been introduced, which applied, however, only to
cities, towns, and boroughs, unless they were extended to any shire at the request of its Council :
the definition of a factory was amended so as to
include all places in which four white men or two
Chinamen were employed in manufacturing goods
for sale ; such places had to be registered, subject to
the approval of the premises by the Local Council,
and the employers were bound to keep a record
showing the names of the persons employed in the
factory, the sort of work done by them, and the
names and addresses of outside workers ; the employment of children under thirteen years of age
was prohibited ; machinery had to be fenced in in
order to prevent accidents, and persons in charge of
steam-engines and boilers, with a few exceptions,
had to obtain certificates of competency. As regards
the enforcement of these and other provisions, inspectors were authorised to enter a factory at any
reasonable time, to make any pertinent inquiry and
examination, to demand the production of any
certificate or documents kept in pursuance of the
Act, and, generally, to exercise such other powers as
might be necessary for carrying it into effect. Proceedings for offences against the Act were to be
taken before two or more justices, who, upon a
conviction, would be guided by a prescribed scale
of fines and penalties. Finally, retail shops were

dealt with by a provision which limited the hours during which they might be kept open ; but certain categories of shops were explicitly excluded, and Municipal Councils were given the power of altering the hours upon a petition of a majority of the shopkeepers.

The absence of finality in such legislation was soon shown by the demand for further restrictions, which was met by the Government by the customary expedient of the appointment of a Royal Commission. The census of 1891 had given the number of persons employed in connection with the manufacturing industries as 96,000, of whom less than a half were in registered factories. The remainder were working in shires, in laundries and dye works, in workrooms other than Chinese in which less than four persons were employed, or in their own homes. The Commission consequently, in the pursuance of their instructions to "inquire and report as to the working of the Factories and Shops Act, 1890, with regard to the alleged existence of the practice known as sweating and the alleged insanitary condition of factories and workrooms," had a wide field of investigation, but turned their attention principally to the industries in which the circumstances of the workers were believed to be most unfavourable. In the clothing industry they found that, beyond the common grievance of slackness of trade, those employed in factories had little to complain of in the matter of

wages, but that among the outworkers, owing to
the depression, competition had reduced the rate of
pay to the lowest level compatible with continued
existence. They were informed of many cases,
which have been corroborated by factory inspectors
and others, of women who, working from twelve to
fourteen hours a day, were unable to earn more
than ten or twelve shillings in a week. It was contended that, as in other countries, the competition
was rendered more acute by those who were not
dependent upon the work for a livelihood. Another
result of this competition was seen in the policy
pursued by several large firms which had closed
factories built at a heavy cost and were relying
upon their operations being carried on by contractors, because they had been unable to produce
goods at the factory at the rate at which they could
be turned out by those who employed the services
of outworkers. An attempt had been made by the
women to protect their interests by the formation
of a Tailoresses' Union, which, after a fitful existence, collapsed in 1893. Since that time, in the
absence of any form of combination, contractors
had been able to play off the outworkers against
the inworkers and against each other. It may here
be noted that, according to a recent report of the
Chief Inspector of Factories, the inquiry caused
the rate of payment to be lowered in consequence
of the publicity given to the very small wages paid
by some firms engaged in the clothing trade.

In the course of their inquiries into the furniture trade, the Commissioners found that the Chinese, by evasions of the Factory Act, their poor way of living, long hours of labour and acceptance of low wages, had practically ruined the European cabinet-makers. Their competition was confined to that branch of the industry, but had indirectly affected it as a whole. Statistics showed that in 1886 there were 64 registered European furniture factories employing 1,022 male hands, while in 1894 the number of factories had decreased to 46 and of employés to 320. On the other side, the number of Chinese employed as carpenters and cabinetmakers had increased from 66 in 1880 to 320 in 1886, and decreased to 246 in 1894. It appeared that the Chinese, having ousted the European workmen from the industry, had engaged in a keen competition among themselves, which had reduced prices to such a low level that many manufacturers had been compelled to close their factories and dismiss their workmen. These latter had commenced to make articles of furniture on their own account, and were reputed to be in a pitiable state of destitution. The Commissioners came to the conclusion that, while the unsatisfactory condition of trade had contributed to the distress of the European cabinetmakers, the competition of the Chinese had been the greatest factor in bringing about the existing state of affairs.

Their recommendations were embodied in a

measure introduced in 1895 and passed in the following session, but limited in its operation, by the action of the Council, to a period of four years. Its most important provisions aim at the protection of the workers in those industries in which they are least able to protect themselves. The desire of the Government was to get persons as far as possible to work in factories and to deal with the difficulty of outworkers by a system of permits. Clause 13 of the Bill prohibited the making up of apparel outside a factory except by those who had received a permit from the chief inspector, which was not to be given unless he were satisfied that the person applying for it was prevented by domestic duties or bodily affliction from working inside a factory or workroom. Employers were to keep a record showing the work done by holders of permits, their names and addresses, and the amount of remuneration, which was to be forwarded periodically to the chief inspector, and might be published in the Government Gazette at the discretion of the Governor in Council. The number of outworkers would be reduced to a minimum, and the fear of publicity would act as a check upon their employers. A further protection was afforded to makers of furniture and of clothing or wearing apparel, including boots and shoes, by clauses under which the Governor in Council was authorised to appoint special Boards, consisting of a chairman and four members, of whom two were to be representatives

of occupiers of factories and workrooms in which
such articles were prepared or manufactured, and
two of the persons employed in wholly or partly
preparing such articles. The Board was to determine the lowest rate which should be paid to the
employés, whether working inside or outside a
factory. The Assembly added another clause which
authorised the appointment of similar Boards for
the determination of the hours of labour in any
manufacturing industry, but the Council refused to
accept it, and also rejected the clause which prohibited outside work by others than holders of
permits. They introduced amendments which
provided that the discretionary publication of
particulars in the Gazette should be limited to
cases in which an employer had been convicted
for some contravention of the Factories and Shops
Acts, and that the special Wage Boards should be
elective, in the belief that it would be dangerous
to vest the power of appointment in the Governor
in Council, since it would actually be exercised by
the Chief Secretary. The Government agreed to the
former of these amendments, as the value of the
right of publication was lessened by the Council's
acceptance of the principle of the Wage Boards; but
upon the other points of difference a conflict ensued
between the two Houses, which resulted in the final
decision that the Boards are to be elective, and that
outworkers will not be required to obtain a permit,
but, if engaged in the manufacture of clothing or

wearing apparel, must register their names and addresses with the chief inspector, for the confidential use of the Department, and must answer all questions put to them by inspectors as to the names of their employers and the rate of remuneration. The Chief Secretary had explained in the Assembly that the Government desired to obtain the registration of outworkers in order that they might know from the individuals themselves the addresses at which they were working, and whether they were being paid in accordance with the prices fixed by the Boards. It is also provided that a sub-contractor, equally with the occupier of a factory, must keep the prescribed record of all work given out by him.

The furniture trade, as has been seen, is one of those for which the Governor in Council may cause special Boards to be elected; but it has been realised that, in the cabinet-making branch, owing to their superior numbers, the Chinese would obtain a controlling voice. This difficulty was met by an amending Bill which authorised the nomination of these Boards. Other sections of the Act also aim at the protection of the white workman: one Chinaman is to be deemed to constitute a factory, and no person employed in a factory or workroom in the manufacture of any article of furniture is to work on a Sunday, after two o'clock on a Saturday, or between five o'clock in the evening and half-past seven in the morning on any other day of the week. Furniture made in Victoria is to be stamped legibly and indelibly in such a manner as to show whether it was manufactured by white or Chinese labour. It is noteworthy that, through the Boards which will fix the minimum rate of pay in the baking and furniture trades, the Victorian Government are making their first attempt to regulate the labour of men ; in the other trades affected by these Boards women form the vast majority of the workers.

The general provisions of this Act as they affect factories include greater stringency in the sanitary requirements, in the limitation of the hours of labour of women and boys, and in the precautions against accidents. Laundries and dye-works are constituted factories, and the powers of inspectors are in several respects strengthened.

The sections dealing with shops also deserve a word of notice. The necessity for further legislation was based by the Chief Secretary on the ground that under the existing law Municipal Councils were not bound to give effect to petitions received from a majority of shopkeepers, and could only bind their own districts. Besides, the penalties imposed for contravention of any law or bye-law had, in many cases, been so small that shopkeepers had been able to ignore it with practical impunity. He therefore proposed that petitions should in future be addressed either to the Governor or to the local authorities, that a metropolitan district should be constituted so as to render possible uniformity in the hours of closing shops, and that the penalties should be on a fixed scale. These proposals were embodied in the Act, as were others which provided that assistants in shops should have a weekly half-holiday, and that women and boys should not be employed for more than a fixed number of hours in a week or day, nor for more than five hours without an interval for meals, and should have the use of adequate sitting accommodation. These provisions, however, were not to apply to the categories of shops excluded from the operation of previous Acts unless extended to them under regulations made by the Governor in Council. Soon after the passage of the Act a strong feeling arose among the shopkeepers of Melbourne and its suburbs that, as assistants had to receive a weekly half-holiday, shops should be closed upon one afternoon in the week ; but opinions differed as to whether the day should be Saturday or Wednesday. The shopkeepers in the city were disposed to favour the former, those in the suburbs were divided in their views.

The Act should be regarded as a humane attempt to minimise the sufferings of the outworkers and to improve the conditions of labour of the toiling masses of the population. The appointment of the special Boards is regarded with sympathy even by those who doubt the possibility of enforcing a minimum wage in the case of persons whose competition is intensified by the fear of starvation. Two general considerations suggest themselves : that a vast discretionary power is vested in the Executive, and that the inspectors will be confronted with a task of hopeless magnitude. On the first point it is to be noted that the Governor in Council, acting naturally upon the advice of the Chief Secretary, may not only exercise the powers already mentioned, but may extend the provisions of the Act or any of them to any shire or part of a shire, and make regulations upon a large number of subjects connected with the efficient administration of all the Factories and Shop Acts. As regards the inspectors, who are eleven in number, it is to be feared that, though they may invite the co-operation of the police, they will be unable adequately to supervise factories, watch the labour of the single Chinaman, protect the home-worker from the tyranny of the contractor, and assure to assistants in shops the conditions to which they are legally entitled. They will undoubtedly be fettered by the unwillingness of the workers to supply information which may lead to the loss of their employment.

The correlative of protection, which principally benefits the manufacturer, is the direct encouragement of the enterprise of the producer. In this respect successive Governments have displayed an eagerness which has not always been confined within the limits of prudence. The borrowed capital sunk in the construction and equipment of the Victorian Railways is about £36,730,000, which returned in the year 1895–6 a net profit on working of £855,000, being a deficit of £584,000 upon £1,439,000, the

annual charge for interest upon the loans; but a
large proportion of this deficiency was due to the
failure of the wheat crop and the consequent
decrease in the amount of goods carried along the
lines. Recent returns show that several lines not
only do not pay any interest on the capital expenditure, but do not earn even as much as is disbursed
in working expenses. The report of the Railway
Inquiry Board shows that the Assembly was actually
disposed at one time to sanction the expenditure of
a further sum of £41,000,000 upon the construction
of new lines; but the *Age* newspaper published a
series of articles which showed clearly that national
insolvency would follow the approval of expenditure
on such a gigantic scale. The exposure attained its
object, but involved the proprietor, Mr. David Syme,
in actions for libel, brought by the Railway Commissioners, which extended, with intervals, over a
period of four years. Finally, he was proved to have
been entirely justified in his language, but was
saddled with an enormous bill of costs as the reward
of his patriotic efforts on behalf of the community.
The danger that similar proposals might be carried
in the future was lessened in 1890, when the Standing
Committee was appointed as a check upon the
extravagant tendencies and culpable pliability of
individual members.

Again, in connection with water supply and
irrigation, the expenditure has been on an extravagant scale. The Melbourne Waterworks are

justified by the requirements of the metropolis, but those of Geelong and of Bendigo and adjacent areas commenced in 1865, and constructed at a capital cost of £1,427,000, show an annual deficit of £35,000 ; and other national works which cost £830,000 are dependent for a return upon irrigation trusts, most of which are unable to meet their own liabilities. Apart from this direct expenditure, the State has advanced £2,438,000 to local bodies, urban and rural waterworks trusts and irrigation trusts. Adding together these different amounts, we find the total direct and indirect expenditure of the State to have been £4,695,000, and we learn from the report of a recent Royal Commission that the annual revenue is about £68,000, or less than 1½ per cent. upon the capital. As the money bears an average interest of 4 per cent., the loss to the consolidated revenue is at the rate of £120,000 a year. The expenditure was based upon the principle that the national credit should be pledged in order that farmers and land and property owners might be assisted to provide works of water supply which would accelerate the permanent settlement of many parts of the Province. Loans had been granted to municipalities before 1881, but in that year the question was treated comprehensively by the Water Conservation Act, which authorised the constitution of trusts for the construction of works of water supply for domestic purposes and the use of stock. In 1883 the Act was amended so as to include trusts formed for the promotion of works of irrigation. The Urban Trusts and local bodies generally have met their obligations satisfactorily, with the exception of some of the latter, which, instead of striking higher rates or increasing the charge for the water, appear to have hoped that the State would step in and relieve them of their liabilities. The Rural and Irrigation Trusts also have attempted to throw the duty of paying interest on the cost of the works upon the taxpayers of the whole province. In the latter case the Public Works Department cannot be absolved from blame. It is clear from the report of the Commission that money was advanced to Irrigation Trusts without an adequate preliminary investigation of the amount of water available or of the number of settlers who would make use of it. "The public mind was excited at the time, and the gospel of irrigation was preached from one end of the Colony to the other. The farmers had been suffering from a cycle of dry seasons, the price of produce was high, and the prospect of insuring their crops against the exigencies of climate by means of irrigation appears to have overruled all prudential considerations. Schemes were hastily conceived and as hastily carried out. The question as to whether the cost of the undertaking would be commensurate with the benefits to be derived therefrom, or whether the land could bear the burden that would be placed upon it, was apparently lightly considered, if considered at all." But, according to an official who had been concerned in the matter, the Department, far from readily concurring in or urging on schemes, had done its utmost to restrain the popular enthusiasm. Continued pressure had been exercised by deputations, generally supported by the Member for the district, which tried to induce Ministers to set aside formalities in view of the great necessity for water and of the great benefit that would ensue. The lavishness of the Department, whatever may have been its cause, was equalled by that of the Trusts, which in most cases expended the loan money as expeditiously as possible without regard to the requirements of the district or the supervision of the undertakings ; they did not realise that they would ever be called upon to provide for meeting the interest on the moneys advanced to them. There can be no doubt that the Government overrated the knowledge and ability of the Trusts, and their recognition of the responsibility involved in the control of large sums of public money. The Royal Commissioners recommended that, after Parliament had decided what concessions should be made, the enforcement of the monetary obligations should be transferred from the Department to the Audit Commissioners, who should be vested with powers enabling them to take action to recover arrears due to the State. They believed that, in the absence of such a change, the Department, being subject to political pressure, might make further concessions, and again allow matters to drift into an unsatisfactory condition.

The next instance of national expenditure in the promotion of enterprise comes under a different category : the State has, since 1878, devoted to the encouragement of the gold-mining industry the sum of £800,000, which was not intended to give a direct return upon the outlay so much as to maintain the pre-eminence of Victoria among the gold-producing Provinces of Australasia. Of this amount £455,000 was expended in boring, the remainder in subsidies to mining companies and prospecting parties. But, as in the case of railways and works of water supply, the Government were confronted by the extreme difficulty of providing safeguards against the misapplication of the funds. Direct control by the Minister of Mines was proved neither to yield good results nor to be satisfactory to the Minister, as he was subjected to continual pressure from Members of Parliament. Prospecting Boards were, accordingly, appointed in the seven mining districts into which the Province is divided, each Board consisting of five members, the surveyor of the district, a member of the Mine-owners' Association, a member of the Miners' Association, a member of the local mining board, and a representative of the municipalities. These men were authorised to allocate all votes, and, according to a statement of the present Minister, as they represented different interests in the mining and different localities, they took a parochial view of their duties and developed " a kind of unconscious log-rolling " which caused the grants, in many cases, to be devoted to entirely unprofitable objects. The expenditure of the £800,000 is believed to have been of the greatest value to several mining companies, but has produced a direct return of only £11,526, an amount which would have been smaller had not the Minister threatened dividend-paying companies with the forfeiture of their leases unless they repaid their loans to the State.

The Government have also attempted to increase the export of such articles as butter, wine, cheese, and frozen meat, for which a large market is believed to be obtainable in Great Britain. Their policy has been to foster these industries by means of bonuses to producers, subsidies to owners of factories, and the free use of cold storage at refrigerating works, and to enforce a certain standard of quality as a necessary condition of their assistance. As the industry progresses the bonus is reduced and finally withdrawn, and charges are made for cold storage which are sufficient to reimburse the State for its outlay. Such a course has already been pursued in the most successful case, that of butter, in which the value of the amount annually exported has risen from £51,000 in 1889–90 to £876,000 in 1895–6. In this manner the State is not permanently engaged, but initiates its expenditure at the highest point and gradually releases itself from the obligation.

In 1893 the Government were confronted with

a large amount of misery among the working classes, much of it undeserved, which had resulted from the collapse of many land companies and banking and building associations. An artificial prosperity, caused by the inflation of metropolitan values, had created a demand for the services of a disproportionate number of artisans, who, upon the inevitable reaction, were thrown suddenly out of employment. Under these circumstances the Ministry were called upon to do something to relieve the distress, and passed a new Land Act which offered favourable terms, in the way of tenure and monetary advances, to those who were willing to settle upon the land. They were enabled to take it up either individually or in associations of not less than six persons who desired to live near each other. At the expiration of a year after the passage of the Act 4,080 applications had been received, of which 2,122 had been approved, 993 rejected, and 965 were under consideration ; and, in order that the benefit might be immediate, the land had been made available as speedily as possible and applicants had not been compelled to wait until blocks had been surveyed. In view of the conditions under which the settlements were formed it is not surprising to learn from subsequent official reports that the favourable anticipations have, in numerous instances, not been realised, owing to the unsuitability of the soil, the inexperience or physical incapacity of the settlers, or the absence of a local demand for labour or of a market for the surplus produce. Many of the associations have been disbanded as the members were unable to work together harmoniously ; and those that are still in existence have, in almost every case, abandoned the co-operative principle and are working their blocks on individual lines. In 1896 the number of resident settlers was 2,127, who, with their wives and families, formed a total population of 8,802 ; they had received, during the three years, advances from the Government to the amount of £57,000.

The Act of 1893 also provided for the establishment of Labour Colonies. The movement in this direction originated with a few people at Melbourne, who saw the futility of periodical doles to the destitute, which were of merely temporary assistance to them and did not place them in the way of earning a permanent livelihood. It was also felt that, in the absence of any system similar to the English poor-law, which, whatever its evils, relieves the conscience of the community, ministers were subject to continual pressure, which compelled them to institute public works for the sole benefit of the unemployed. In 1892 the distress was met, as far as the public were concerned, by the subscription of a large sum of money, which was distributed through the agency of the local branch of the Charity Organisation Society ; but, in the following year, the distress being still more acute, the idea of a Labour Colony rapidly gained ground and was met by the Government by the grant of an area of 800 acres at Leongatha, some 80 miles from Melbourne, which enabled the promoters of the scheme at one to commence their operations. At the outset it had been intended that the funds should be obtained, partly by private subscription, partly by *pro-rata* contributions from the national exchequer ; but, in the absence of popular response, the Government deemed it advisable, at the commencement of 1894, to take over the entire administration of the colony, and appointed, as Honorary Superintendent, Colonel Goldstein, who had been actively identified with the undertaking. Colonel Goldstein states that the main purpose of the colony, which is based on a German model, is to give temporary work at unattractive wages to the able-bodied unemployed in order that they may be prevented from passing over the narrow line which separates poverty from pauperism. At first the aged and infirm were admitted, but it was found that employment could not be obtained for them and that their presence affected the value of the colony as a means of instruction for a class of men in whom it is necessary to arouse a spirit of responsible independence. They are, moreover, provided for by benevolent asylums and other charitable institutions which receive large subsidies from the Government. Consequently men beyond the age of 55 years are now only received in exceptional cases. All applicants are registered, and, if their alleged destitution is believed to be genuine, are forwarded by rail to the colony, where they receive free board and lodging. The colonists are subjected to strict discipline, work for a week without pay upon probation, and then earn wages which rise to a maximum of 4s. a week; they receive no money while at the colony, but may draw certain necessaries, or, if married, cause their wages to be remitted to their wives. The work is so arranged that the capabilities of the colonists may be used to the best advantage and that they may be fitted as far as possible for agricultural employment, which is obtained for them by means of a Labour Bureau established at the colony. At the expiration of six months, or upon an accumulation in their favour of a credit balance amounting to 30s., colonists must, subject to occasional exemptions, seek employment elsewhere, and may not be re-admitted under a period of six weeks. In this manner the men either obtain outside employment while resident at the colony or leave it possessed of a sum of money which renders them better able to search for it; they have the alternative of applying subsequently for re-admittance. The results obtained during the three years have been of a most satisfactory character; 1,832 men have passed through the colony since its inception, of whom only 124 have been dismissed for faults, and none for insubordination; 573 have had remunerative work found for them, and the remainder have earned sufficient ready money to enable them to set out in search of employment. There have been 566 re-admissions of 307 men who have returned from one to eight times. " The majority of the men," says Colonel Goldstein, "are of the shiftless sort, who cannot do anything for themselves. As Leongatha is 80 miles from Melbourne, we seldom see the genuine loafer there. The men who go are willing enough to work when shown how, but they seem unable to rouse themselves into any sort of vigour, to say nothing of enthusiasm, until they have been there a considerable time. . . . Numerous instances could be given indicative of the generally helpless nature of the men. There can be no doubt that employers, during the depression, will first reduce their worst men. Of these, many have sufficient energy to shift for themselves ; the rest drift to the labour colony. Most of them have suffered severely from privation and poverty, and probably have had their dejected condition further dispirited by semi-starvation. . . . After a few months' stay it is surprising to see the difference in their appearance, and, what is more to the purpose, their discovery that a new kind of life is opened to them. Bush-work gives them a healthier feeling of self-dependence than they ever enjoyed before, especially so for men who have a trade behind them ready when the chance comes." The total outlay has amounted to £11,276, which has been expended mainly upon farm appointments, implements, and permanent improvements, and is represented by assets of the value of £10,861. The net cost must be regarded as exceedingly small in view of the fact that, as the great majority of the colonists are artisans and quite unused to bush or farm work, their labour is necessarily slow and expensive, and that, as soon as a man begins to be useful, he is selected for some private employer. The Labour Colony has, it is maintained, apart from the benefits conferred upon hundreds of individuals, paralysed the agitation of the unemployed; as long as it is in existence no able-bodied man need starve.

Finally, a measure, passed in 1896, aimed at the protection of pastoralists, farmers, and other cultivators of the soil by providing machinery by which the State might grant loans to them, upon adequate security, at a low rate of interest, with a sinking fund extending over a long period of years.

The salient features of Victorian legislation are the strong note of humanity and the confidence in the wisdom and efficiency of State action. If this confidence has sometimes been misplaced, there is no reason to suppose that the Victorians have imposed upon themselves a burden that they are unable to bear. They are an energetic race, who have not only developed the resources of their own country, but have obtained large interests in New South Wales and Queensland. If in the past they were too much inclined to draw bills upon futurity, they have had a sharp lesson which has taught them the necessity of retrenchment and compelled them to reduce their annual expenditure by a third of the total amount. It is impossible to form an unfavourable estimate of the prospects, or of the high average prosperity, of a population of less than 1,200,000 persons, which includes 185,000 freeholders and has accumulated at the Savings Banks £7,300,000 divided among nearly 340,000 depositors.

VI

THE GROWTH AND DEVELOPMENT OF WESTERN AUSTRALIA

Constitutional history—The relations of Church and State—Natural impediments to development—The construction of railways—The scarcity of water—The promotion of the mining and other industries—The absence of parties in Parliament.

WESTERN AUSTRALIA received the privileges of Responsible Government many years after the other Australasian Provinces ; otherwise, its constitutional development has proceeded upon similar lines. The first Governor was appointed in 1829, and administered the affairs of the country with the assistance of an Executive Council. Two years later a Legislative Council was established which consisted solely of the members of the Executive Council, but it was subsequently widened by the admission, at first, of unofficial nominee members, afterwards of a sufficient number of elected members to form a majority of the whole body. Then an agitation sprang up in the Province in favour of Responsible Government, and in 1889, after a unanimous vote of the Legislative Council, a Constitution Bill was submitted by the Government, considered by the Council, and forwarded to the Secretary of State for the Colonies. In the House of Commons it met with considerable opposition, on the ground that the Crown Lands of the Province should not be handed over to a population of only 46,000 persons. But, upon a favourable report of a Select Committee and representation made by the Agents-General of the other Australasian Provinces, the point was decided in the sense desired by the Province, and, as the Bill passed rapidly through the House of Lords, it received the Royal Assent in August, 1890.

Under the Constitution the Executive power is vested in the Governor, who acts by the advice of a Cabinet composed of five responsible Ministers. They are, at the present time, the Colonial Treasurer and Colonial Secretary, the Attorney-General, the Commissioner of Railways and Director of Public Works, the Commissioner of Crown Lands, and the Minister of Mines. The Premier, Sir John Forrest, holds the offices of Colonial Secretary and Colonial Treasurer, and the Minister of Mines, the only Minister in the Upper House, controls the Postal and Telegraphic Departments.

The Legislative authority is vested in the two Houses of Parliament, the Legislative Council and the Legislative Assembly. The Council consists of twenty-one members, of whom a third retire every two years. They are elected upon a property qualification, and must have been resident for at least two years in the Province. The Assembly consists of thirty-three members, who must have resided at least one year in the Province, and are elected upon a wider franchise for the period of four years. No remuneration is paid to the members of either House, but they receive free passes over all Government Railways and, by courtesy, over those belonging to private companies.

The limitations upon the power of legislation possessed by the Parliament of Western Australia are similar to those imposed upon the Legislatures of other Australian Provinces, except that the protection of the aborigines has been placed in the hands of an independent Board, nominated and controlled by the Governor. It receives for the execution of its duties 1 per cent. of the annual revenue of the country, but cannot carry them out without the active support of Government officials. The existence of this Board is strongly resented by Western Australians as an unjust reflection upon them, and as an imputation that they cannot be trusted to deal in a just and humane manner towards the natives ; and the Premier, voicing the unanimous opinion of both Houses, has attempted, hitherto without success, to secure the repeal of the obnoxious section of the Constitution Act.

The attitude of the Government in regard to the relations between Church and State as affecting the endowment of religious bodies and the assistance given to denominational schools was, until recently, that grants should annually be voted by Parliament. But the trend of public opinion has been in the direction of secular education and the termination of the payments made to the Churches. The matter was, accordingly, during the session of 1895, dealt with by the Ecclesiastical Grants Abolition Act and the Assisted Schools Abolition Act. Previously the payments to the Churches had been at the rate of about £3,500 per annum, of which the Church of England received £2,000, the Roman Catholics £1,000, and the Wesleyans and Presbyterians £360 and £160 respectively. The grants have been commuted at ten years' purchase, and the capital amount is to be paid *pro rata* out of the Consolidated Revenue Fund in two equal instalments to the recognised heads of each religious denomination. This Bill was passed, with universal approval, through both Houses of Parliament, but a like unanimity was not manifested in regard to the Education question. In fact, early in the session, the Premier had stated that he had no immediate intention of dealing with it, but his hands were forced by popular opinion, as manifested by the result of several elections fought upon that issue. Consequently, after a resolution passed by both Houses that " It is expedient that the Assisted " (denominational) " Schools should no longer form part of the public Educational system of the Colony," and on the report of a Joint Committee, a Bill was introduced by the Premier into the

Assembly fixing the sum to be paid as compensation, in lieu of grants in aid, at £20,000. In 1894 one-third of the children being educated in the Colony were attending the Assisted Schools, at a cost to the country of £2,093 for the Assisted, and £11,356 for the Government Schools. The Bill was hotly discussed ; the Opposition divided over the amount, and were only beaten by one vote, and it was finally decided that the compensation should be £15,000. The whole of this money will be paid to the Roman Catholics, who had alone taken advantage of the system. There is a High School at Perth established by statute ; otherwise little has been done in the direction of secondary education, and Western Australia has no University. The advantages of primary education have been extended as far as possible ; any district which can guarantee the attendance of fifteen children can claim the erection of a school and the appointment of a teacher ; but it is clear that, in a very sparsely inhabited country, no system can be devised which will reach the whole population.

The policy of the Ministry has been, in the main, one of loans and public works. They were called upon, at the inauguration of Responsible Government, to administer an area of nearly a million square miles, thinly populated and penalised by great natural drawbacks, such as the scarcity of good harbours, the difficulty of inland communication, and the absence over large tracts of country of a sufficient supply of water. These drawbacks the Government have, in various ways, done their best to overcome.

The principal ports of Western Australia are—on the south Albany and Esperance Bay, on the west Bunbury, Fremantle, and Geraldtown, and on the north-west Cossack and Broome. The most important of these are Albany, a fine natural harbour, which is the point of call of the ocean liners, and Fremantle, the port of Perth. All have been improved, as far as conditions would permit, by dredging operations and the construction of piers and jetties, but very extensive works, for which the sum of £350,000 has already been allotted, are being carried out at Fremantle, in the hope of making it a good and commodious harbour for all classes of ocean vessels. In the interests of safe navigation, lighthouses have been erected at various points along the coast.

As the rivers are mostly filled only during the rainy season, and unnavigable for any distance even for small boats, the methods of internal transit are limited to road and rail. The Government have regarded the construction of roads as a matter of national rather than of purely local importance, and have expended upon them large sums of money. They are at present engaged in opening up stock routes to the North and between the Murchison and Coolgardie Goldfields. Their railway policy has been to render accessible the different resources of the country. The South-Western Railway from Perth to Bunbury, Busselton, and Donnybrook traverses country suitable for the growth of cereals and for mixed farming. Its course is along the foot of the Darling Range, which is covered with valuable forests of jarrah. Parliament has recently sanctioned two extensions : to Collie, an important coalfield, and to Bridgetown, the centre of an agricultural area. The Eastern Railway, starting from Fremantle, passes through Perth and taps an important district adapted for general agriculture, fruit-growing, and viticulture ; it connects with the Yilgarn Railway, which has now been completed to several points upon the Coolgardie Goldfields, and will be dependent for its returns upon their prosperity, as it passes through vast areas of arid scrub. The Northern Railway consists of short lines from Geraldtown, which pass through country suitable, in parts, for the growth of cereals, in others, for pastoral purposes ; it is to be continued to Cue, on the Murchison Goldfield. The above are all Government railways, built under private contract and equipped and managed by the State. There are also two large private companies, the Great Southern Railway, connecting Albany with Beverley, the terminus of the Eastern Railway, and the Midland Railway, connecting Geraldtown with Perth at points on the Northern and Eastern Railways. They were built upon the land-grant system, at a time when the Government were anxious to extend the railways, but were not in a position to incur the cost of their construction. This system is not likely to be adopted again, as both Companies have pursued an ungenerous policy in regard to the alienation of their lands, while the Midland Company were unable to complete their undertaking without the assistance of the Government, which, in return for a mortgage of the whole line, guaranteed for them the interest and principal of a loan of £500,000. In fact, during the session of 1896, the Government, after negotiations with the Great Southern Railway Company, obtained the authority of Parliament for the negotiation of a loan for the purchase of all its interests, including the permanent way, rolling stock, buildings, and unsold lands.

In the southern and western portions of the Province water is plentiful. The northern portion is subject to terrible drought, such as that which a few years ago almost ruined the squatters and caused the loss of three-quarters of a million sheep. But the attention of the Government has been mainly turned to the eastern division, which includes the Yilgarn, Coolgardie, and Dundas Goldfields, and has an average annual rainfall of about ten inches, and it is in this portion of the country that the heaviest expenditure was incurred during the year ending June 30, 1895. Thirteen large and two small tanks were completed on the Coolgardie Goldfields with a capacity of 13½ millions of gallons and at a total cost of nearly £38,000. Wells were sunk, bores put down in the search for water, condenser plants erected, and new soaks opened up at advantageous places throughout the district. Wells have also been sunk, and reservoirs constructed, on the Murchison and Pilbarra Goldfields, and in other parts of the country. But the greatest undertaking in this direction will be the construction of vast works for the supply from a distance of water to the Coolgardie Goldfields. Parliament has authorised the required loan, and may therefore be presumed to concur with the Ministry in the belief that the necessary water cannot be obtained on the spot by artesian bores or otherwise. The future of Western Australia is bound up with that of the goldfields. Should they fail through lack of water, recent immigrants would leave the country, and their departure would cripple, if not ruin, the agricultural industry, and cause immediately a heavy fall in the revenue. Under these circumstances, the scheme of the Government, even though it entails a very large expenditure, might be justified as being essential to the continued prosperity of the Province. A similar argument may be applied to the large sums spent upon the railways, since they, as well as the waterworks, should be remunerative ; but when we find Parliament sanctioning, in one session, applications for loans amounting to seven millions —and bear in mind the smallness of the population —we cannot but fear that the Province is beginning to borrow recklessly and may expose itself to the financial troubles which have overtaken some of its Eastern neighbours.

So much for the natural difficulties and the attempts made, and about to be made, by the Government to overcome them; but they have recognised that the heavy expenditure upon public works would be unjustifiable in the absence of simultaneous efforts to encourage the occupation and cultivation of the land and the development of the mineral resources; and they have, therefore, while not embarking upon a policy of direct subsidies for the payment of the passages of immigrants, offered every inducement to people to come to the Province of their own accord. Intending settlers or companies can obtain, upon favourable terms, land for pastoral or agricultural purposes, mineral leases, and concessions giving them the right to cut timber upon the State forests. A miner can acquire, on the annual payment of ten shillings, a miner's right, entitling him to take possession of, mine, and occupy, unoccupied Crown Lands for gold mining in accordance with the Mining Regulations. The general conditions dealing with the alienation of Crown Lands are laid down in the Land Regulations, under which the Province has been divided into six districts, in order that different terms may be made in accordance with the varying quality and capabilities of the soil in different parts of the country. Pastoral leases may be obtained at a rent ranging from five shillings to £1 a year for 1,000 acres.

Agricultural land is in most parts of the country sold at ten shillings an acre, to be paid either directly or by annual instalments ; but the title to the land is not given until certain stated improvements have been carried out upon it, in order to prevent its being held in an unimproved condition for speculative purposes, and residence is encouraged by the enforcement of a larger expenditure in improvements upon occupiers who do not live upon their estates. As a further inducement to settlers, the Government have set apart special agricultural areas, which they cause to be surveyed before selection and marked out in blocks ; they offer, under the Homesteads Act, 1893, free grants of land not exceeding 160 acres in extent, subject to stringent conditions as to residence and expenditure upon improvements ; and they have established an agricultural bank which is authorised to make advances to farmers and other cultivators of the soil. The policy of the Government has had considerable success, as the total area of cultivated land rose from 86,000 acres in 1886 to 193,000 acres at the end of 1894. But farmers have had to contend with great difficulties in the work and expense required for the clearing of the land, and in the absence of a market for their produce. A distinct improvement, however, has obtained since the advent of a large population upon the goldfields, whose wants they may hope to supply.

It must be admitted that Sir John Forrest and his colleagues have had matters entirely in their favour.

The credit of the Province has steadily improved, in view of its mining operations ; for the same reason the railways have shown the most satisfactory returns, and the receipts from the Customs, under a tariff levied primarily for purposes of revenue, but partially protective in its incidence, have increased by leaps and bounds. Again, in Parliament the Ministry have met with but little opposition. Upon the inauguration of Responsible Government, the Premier had the prestige of former office under the Crown, and found himself face to face with an Assembly which had no experience in the principles of Party Government. The members were intimately acquainted with each other, and criticism of the Ministry was resented as a personal insult. The so-called Opposition made no serious attempt to overthrow the Government, partly because, in the dearth of men of both ability and leisure, there was no material for the formation of an alternative Ministry ; partly because they were in agreement with them upon most of the questions that came up for discussion. The policy of the construction of public works out of loans was generally acceptable, and soon justified itself by results, owing, to a great extent, to the development of the goldfields. Mines had been worked in Western Australia for a considerable time, but attracted little attention until the great discoveries at Coolgardie and in its neighbourhood. These came at a most opportune moment. A large amount of capital in Europe was seeking profitable employment ; the stagnation of business in the Eastern Provinces of Australia had brought hardship upon the labouring population and made them anxious to seek work elsewhere ; and the success of the South African Mines had caused the British public to look favourably upon mining speculations. As a result, mines were successfully floated in London and in Australia, immigrants poured in from the Eastern Provinces, mercantile firms established branches at Perth and at other centres, and the revenue obtained from the Customs and from the Railways and other public departments increased to an unparalleled extent. But the increase of revenue naturally caused a large increase in the work of the departments concerned, and they failed signally to meet the additional demands upon them.

The Telegraphic and Postal Department obtained an evil pre-eminence through its irregularity and untrustworthiness, and caused much inconvenience and monetary loss, owing to the delay in the delivery of letters and telegrams. Complaints were also rife against the Railway Department, as imported machinery lay for months at Fremantle, because the Government had not sufficient trucks in which to take it up the line to its place of destination. It must be remembered, however, that the public services had been organised to meet the needs of a far smaller population and were called upon to carry out work which had increased at a rapidity which could not be foreseen. A certain amount of difficulty was, under these circumstances, bound to occur, as the Government would not have been justified in launching into heavy additional expenditure until they had reasonable assurance of the permanence of the goldfields and of the consequent increase of business.

Hitherto the Government of Western Australia has been that of a huge land development company ; constitutional questions have been in the background. But a tendency is already perceptible among recent immigrants to demand manhood suffrage, payment of members, and other items of democratic legislation to which they have been accustomed in the Eastern Provinces. This movement, however, will be checked by the conservative instincts of the native population, and by the general belief that the Ministry have guided the destinies of the province wisely during the crucial years which have succeeded the inauguration of Responsible Government.

VII

DISCURSIVE NOTES ON TASMANIA

The restriction of the immigration of coloured races—Betting and lotteries — The adoption of a modification of Hare's System of Voting—Conflicts between the two Houses of Parliament—Finance and taxation—Land Grant Railways.

THE session of the Tasmanian Parliament in 1896 was of a quiet character as far as the Ministerial programme was concerned. Measures were introduced, among others, for the extension to certain coloured races of the restrictions imposed upon the immigration of the Chinese, for the better suppression of public betting and gaming, for the inspection of certain products intended for export, for the consolidation and amendment of the electoral laws, and for the reference to a plebiscite of disputes between the House of Assembly and the Legislative Council.

The first of these measures was introduced in pursuance of a resolution passed at the Premiers' Conference at the commencement of the year, and was based upon the Chinese Immigration Act, 1887, which limits the number of Chinese, not being

British subjects, that may be brought to Tasmania in any vessel in proportion to its tonnage, and throws upon the masters of the vessels the duty of paying a capitation fee of £10 for every such Chinaman that they introduce into the Province. It was proposed to apply this provision to "all male persons belonging to any coloured race inhabiting the Continent of Asia or the Continent of Africa, or any island adjacent thereto, or any island in the Pacific Ocean or Indian Ocean, not being persons duly accredited on any special mission to Her Majesty by the Government or ruler of any country, state, or territory, or to Tasmania under the authority of the Imperial Government." The Bill, which also exempted from its operation the native races of Australia and New Zealand, was accepted by the two Houses of Parliament, but was reserved by the Governor for the Imperial assent, which was likely to be withheld, as the measure would undoubtedly lead to the strongest protests from the Japanese, who will scarcely submit to be treated as an inferior race by an Australian Province. Should this attitude be adopted, a considerable amount of friction may be anticipated, as measures on similar lines have been adopted by the two Houses of Parliament in some of the other Provinces.

The Bill for the better suppression of betting and gaming should rather have been called a Bill for their regulation, as, while it aimed at the entire suppression of book-makers and betting-houses, it did not interfere with the totalisator or with any lotteries which had been authorised by Act of Parliament or were carried on solely by correspondence through the post-office, and in accordance with regulations which might be made by the Governor in Council. The totalisator is now to be found in all the Australasian Provinces except New South Wales and Victoria ; in the latter its adoption has widely been advocated, but has been opposed by the clergy, who have entered into an unconscious alliance with the book-makers. The organisers of the large "Tattersall" Sweeps, which are worked from Tasmania and attract subscribers from all parts of Australasia, will also be unaffected by the Act ; to a certain extent they will even be benefited, as they will be freed from the competition of many of their more humble rivals.

The measure dealing with the inspection of exported produce was deemed advisable on account, partly of the proposed action of other Provinces in regard to Tasmanian fruit, partly of the importance of enabling Tasmanian producers to obtain an official certificate of the quality of their produce. In outside markets, it was contended, in which the Provinces come into competition with each other, dealers gave the preference to, and paid higher prices for, imports which had received the imprimatur of the Government stamp. The interests of the community also would be protected against those of selfish and dishonest traders. It was, therefore, pro-

posed that all dairy produce, fruit, or timber intended
for exportation should be examined by an inspector,
and should not be shipped until he had certified
that it was sound, free from disease, and likely to
reach its destination in a good state of preservation.
The Governor in Council was also authorised to
make regulations for the inspection of the ships
in which such produce was to be carried, for the
protection from unnecessary suffering of live stock
when carried by sea, and for the branding and shipment of products approved of by an inspector for
exportation. The Bill was read a second time in
the Assembly on the understanding that it would be
referred to the persons who would principally be
affected by it, and was so unfavourably received by
them, and especially by the fruit-growers, that it was
shortly afterwards dropped. In several Provinces
inspection has been accompanied by a system of
bonuses to producers, but in this respect Tasmania
has taken no action. Substantial bonuses were,
however, offered some fourteen years ago to manufacturers of considerable quantities of sugar, sacking,
and woollen goods, but of these the last alone has
been claimed.

Tasmania has not followed the example of New
South Wales and South Australia in the adoption of
manhood or adult suffrage and the abolition of
plural votes, but has passed a new Electoral Bill
which adopts a modification of Hare's system, and
thus secures a considerable representation of the

minority in both Houses of Parliament. It provided,
as introduced, that the two principal cities, Hobart
and Launceston, which return, respectively, six and
three, and four and two, representatives to the
Assembly and Council, should thenceforward be
single constituencies, and that "each elector shall
have one vote only, but may vote in the alternative
for as many candidates as he pleases ; and his vote
shall be deemed to be given in the first place for the
candidate opposite whose name in the ballot-paper
the figure 1 is placed ; but in the event of its not
being required to be used for the return of such
candidate, it shall be transferable to the other candidates in succession, in the order of priority indicated
by the figures set opposite their respective names ;
and the elector shall insert opposite the names of
the candidates for whom he wishes to vote, the
figures 1, 2, 3, and so on, in the order of his preference." The method by which the returning
officer was to decide who were the successful candidates was so complicated as to require two pages of
the Bill for its explanation. Briefly stated, it was
as follows : the total number of votes divided by
the number of representatives being the "Quota"
necessary for the election of candidates, the returning officer declares the candidates who have a
number of first votes equal to or greater than the
quota to be elected ; he then notes how many of
the second votes on the papers of the successful
candidates are given to each of the other candidates,

and distributes the surplus votes among them in accordance with their respective proportions. One or more additional candidates are probably thereby elected, and the process is repeated until the requisite number are elected or a further quota is no longer reached. In the latter case, the candidate who has the smallest number of votes is excluded, and the second votes of those who supported him in the first instance are counted to the other candidates. The second votes of the candidates who successively become lowest on the list may be distributed, as often as may be necessary, among the remainder ; in this manner a final result must at length be obtained. The Assembly provided by an amendment that each elector should vote for as many candidates as there were vacancies, while signifying the order of his preference ; the Council reduced the number of requisite votes by one-half, and limited the operation of the Bill to the next general election. A doubt was expressed whether the benefits would counterbalance the additional trouble and inevitable confusion which would attend the first application of the new system. It was also contended that, among a population of not more that 160,000 persons, if the experiment were worthy of a trial, it should be extended to the whole country. The only other electoral peculiarity that I have noted in Australia is to be found in Queensland. Under an Act of 1892 which deals with the election of members of the Assembly, an elector may " indicate on his ballot-paper the name or names of any candidate or candidates for whom he does not vote in the first instance, but for whom he desires his vote or votes to be counted in the event of any candidate or candidates for whom he votes in the first instance not receiving an absolute majority of votes." These contingent votes are not counted unless the requisite number of candidates fail to obtain an absolute majority of all the primary votes ; they are of no value where the candidates are not in the ratio of more than two to one to the vacancies, as it is provided that in such cases the candidates who receive the greatest number of votes shall be elected.

It is a noteworthy fact that the four Provinces, New South Wales, Victoria, South Australia, and Tasmania, which decided in favour of popular election of the delegates to the new Federal Convention and the subsequent approval or rejection of the Draft Constitution by a direct popular vote, are those in which the Ministry advocate a plebiscite for the settlement of disputes between the two Houses of Parliament. The acceptance of the Federation Enabling Bill by the Legislative Councils of these Provinces must weaken the moral force of their opposition to the plebiscite, as it may reasonably be argued that, if the people can be trusted to give an intelligent vote upon the most important of all Australian problems, they can still more be trusted to deal with any question of current politics. In Tasmania Ministers are confronted with a Legislative Council which continually amends, as well as rejects, their financial proposals, justifying its attitude upon the wording of the Constitution Act of 1854. The section in question states that "all Bills for appropriating any part of the revenue or for imposing any tax, rate, duty, or impost shall originate in the House of Assembly, and it shall not be lawful for the House of Assembly to originate or pass any vote, resolution, or Bill for the appropriation of any part of the revenue, or of any tax, rate, duty, or impost for any purpose which shall not have been first recommended by the Governor to the House of Assembly during the session in which such vote, resolution, or Bill shall be passed." As the right of amendment is not specifically withheld, as in the Victorian Constitution, the Legislative Council assumes its possession. The case for the plebiscite was put by the Premier and the Treasurer upon the second reading of the Bill. Sir Edward Braddon stated that the financial privileges of the Assembly had continually been infringed by the Council, and that, on one occasion, in reference to the Drawbacks Bill, they had almost assumed the power of initiating a money vote. Curiously enough, the principal question mentioned by him as suitable for the application of the plebiscite was that of Female Suffrage, which, introduced as a private measure, had been rejected by the Council after he had failed to secure its defeat in the Assembly. In the preceding session, he said, the Assembly had vainly asked the Council to agree to a joint dissolution of both Houses when a Bill had twice been rejected and a General Election had intervened. A similar measure, passed in South Australia in 1881, had operated most successfully, its mere presence on the Statute Book having put an end to the deadlocks which had previously been of constant occurrence. It is probable, however, that the comparative absence of disputes has mainly been due to the democratisation of the Council, which has brought it into close touch with the feeling of the Assembly; and that, in Tasmania, where the electors for the Council are only one in five of those for the Assembly, a joint dissolution would produce little change in the *personnel* of the former body. The Treasurer, Sir Philip Fysh, treating the subject historically, pointed out that the Council had thrown out year after year votes, first passed in 1863, for the expenditure of £103,000 upon the construction of roads and bridges, and had several times rejected the Launceston and Western, Hobart and Launceston, and Mersey and Deloraine Railway Bills. They had three times refused to accept a Bill for the re-assessment of the land of the Province with a view to the imposition of a tax on unimproved values. As regards its opposition to the proposed expenditure of borrowed money upon the construction of railways, roads and bridges, it would appear that the Council in most cases acted wisely, and that the Province would have been benefited if it had persisted in its opposition. The total public debt at the end of June, 1896, was nearly £8,150,000, exclusive of £215,000 in temporary Treasury Bills and £250,000 in Local Inscribed Stock, and entailed an annual liability for interest of £313,000. Towards this amount, the works which should be directly reproductive, such as the railways and the postal and telegraphic services, returned a net revenue, after payment of working expenses, of only £26,000. It may be contended, of course, that the country could not have been developed in the absence of a large expenditure ; but, as the liability forms a heavy burden upon so small a population — a burden, indeed, which might have become almost unbearable but for the valuable discoveries of minerals—the Council seems to have had abundant justification for its efforts to check the extravagant tendencies of the Assembly. The Ministry, after passing the second reading of the Bill in the Assembly by a small majority, withdrew it, as there was no possibility of getting it through the Council ; its introduction appears to have been due to the desire that it should be discussed at the pending General Elections. The principal clause provided that "any Bill which shall be passed by the House of Assembly in two consecutive sessions of Parliament, and which shall be rejected by the Legislative Council in each of

two such consecutive sessions, may be submitted
for the approval of the people of Tasmania by
means of a general poll of, or referendum to, the
electors for the House of Assembly." An interval
of not less than six weeks was to elapse between
the two sessions, and where a Bill had been
amended by the Council, the Assembly was to
be vested with the final decision whether the
amendments effected such substantial alterations
as to be tantamount to a rejection, and might
present an address to the Governor requesting that
a Bill which had been rejected twice or substantially altered might be submitted to a general vote
of the electors. A bare majority of the votes so
recorded was to be sufficient to secure the enactment of the measure subject to the constitutional
rights of the Governor.

The placid progress of the Session was impaired
by the introduction of a private railway Bill, which
led to many nights of contentious debate and much
hostility among the various sections in the Assembly.
All the railways are owned by the State with the
exception of a few short lines in the Northern and
Western portions of the Province which have been
constructed by Mining Companies without any
concessions from the Government. During recent
years the Western district has become an important
mining centre, and should, in the opinion of most
Tasmanians, be connected by railway with either
Launceston or Hobart. But the condition of the

finances is such, as has already been seen, that the Government cannot venture to undertake the construction of further public works unless it can be shown that they will immediately give an adequate return upon the outlay. The small surplus of the last two years was obtained at the cost of rigid retrenchment and high direct taxation, an income tax of eightpence in the pound upon incomes derived from personal exertion, and a shilling upon those derived from property, and a land-tax of a halfpenny in the pound upon the capital value of land. It, therefore, became necessary, if the construction of the line or lines were not to be postponed indefinitely, that the aid of private enterprise should be invoked and that concessions should be offered which would be sufficient to attract private capitalists.

In 1895 a Bill was passed which authorised the Van Diemen's Land Company to construct a railway of about forty miles in length, which would place the West Coast in communication with Emu Bay in the North. At a distance of eighteen miles from the latter place is Ulverstone, which is directly connected with Launceston, and the Government have a balance from loan funds which may be devoted to the construction of a railway across the intervening space. The inducement offered to the Company was the right to mark off, within certain areas, twelve blocks of 320 acres of mineral land, which would be granted to them upon the

completion of the railway. They were limited in
the charges which they might make for the carriage
of passengers and the conveyance of merchandise,
were to pay a royalty of $2\frac{1}{2}$ per cent. upon the
gross value of all minerals obtained by them in
addition to the statutory income tax of one shilling
in the pound, and were to be liable, after the
expiration of twenty-one years, to the resumption
of the railway and all its appurtenances by the
Government at the price of 20 per cent. above the
actual cost of construction. At the end of 1896
the Company had not taken the initial steps
towards the commencement of the undertaking.

The proposal made by a Victorian Syndicate and
submitted to Parliament during the session of 1896,
aimed at the connection by railway of the West
Coast with some point on the State lines in the
South. In return for the construction of the railway, which would be about a hundred miles in
length, the promoters asked for a concession of
large areas of land along its proposed route and
for considerable rights to make use of the rivers
in its vicinity, which are running to waste in the
greatest abundance, as sources of electrical energy.
As the railway would, admittedly, be worked at a
loss for many years, they based their hopes of a
profit upon the probability of the discovery of
minerals and upon the generation of electricity,
which they would either use themselves or dispose
of to companies mining on land belonging to the

State. The district in question, it may be stated, is believed to be of little agricultural value, but to be likely to carry minerals, though it has not adequately been prospected. After its second reading the Bill was referred to a select committee, which made reductions in the concessions, and these were further reduced, after prolonged debate, upon its reconsideration in the Assembly. I have mentioned these details in order to show that, while the State was not in a financial position to undertake the direct construction of railways deemed to be necessary for the development of the resources of the country, the Assembly was not unmindful of the interests of posterity, and sought to reduce the inevitable concessions to the lowest possible point.

VIII

FEMALE SUFFRAGE

I DO not propose, in the present chapter, to discuss the hackneyed arguments for and against female suffrage, but to indicate the progress of the movement in the several Provinces of Australasia, and to note some of the results of the adoption of adult suffrage in South Australia and New Zealand.

As regards the other Provinces, we are bound to consider the existing franchise for the election of members of the Assembly in order to realise what would be the effect of extending it to women upon similar terms. In Victoria manhood suffrage would be superseded by adult suffrage ; in New South Wales and Western Australia, where residence of three and six months, respectively, forms a qualification, the vast majority of women would obtain a place on the rolls ; but in Tasmania and Queensland the right to exercise the franchise would be confined, practically, to widows and women of independent means.

We are also bound to take into consideration the constitution of the Legislative Council in order to gauge the full significance of female suffrage. If it is elective, as the electors must be qualified as freeholders, leaseholders, or occupiers, the vote would be confined to women of independent means and widows or spinsters in personal occupation, and, while the wife and daughters of the poor man would necessarily be excluded from the register, those of the rich man might, as has been done in South Australia, receive special gifts of freehold property which would be sufficient to render them eligible. To this extent, therefore, as in Tasmania and, to a small degree, wherever plural voting is allowed, female suffrage would constitute a new property vote. Similar conditions would not prevail when the members of the Council are nominated upon the recommendation of Ministers who are subject to the control of the popular representatives.

It is probable that Victoria will be the next Province to follow the example of South Australia and New Zealand. A ministerial measure which would have introduced female suffrage, though only in the constituencies of the Assembly, has twice been passed by that House. On the first occasion it was rejected by the Council, on the second it was laid aside on the ground that it had not been approved by the absolute majority which is required in the case of amendments of the constitution. Both Bills were rendered distasteful to the Council by the inclusion of a provision for the abolition of the plural vote, but it is unlikely that the first would, apart from that fact, have been accepted. Many members of the Council, I was told, are favourable to female suffrage, but would have voted in accordance with their opinion that important constitutional changes should not be passed until they have been placed before the electorate. As the life of the Assembly may not exceed three years, the reference need not long be delayed.

In Tasmania, in 1896, the House of Assembly passed a private Bill containing a similar limitation to that in the Victorian measure, and was equally unable to secure the concurrence of the Council. A resolution in favour of female suffrage has been adopted by a large majority in the Assembly of New South Wales, but the question has not been taken up by either of the recognised parties. The Premier may be reckoned as a personal supporter, but declines to move in the matter in view of differences of opinion in the Cabinet. Neither in Western Australia nor in Queensland does the subject arouse much interest.

Such is the state of feeling in five of the six Australian Provinces. In South Australia an arduous contest was concluded in 1894 by the passage of an Act which placed women upon an absolute equality with men in the right to vote for members both of the Assembly and of the Council. It is unnecessary to trace the history of the agitation which may be said to have commenced in 1888 upon the formation of the Women's Franchise League, though a Bill for the enfranchisement of women of property had previously been introduced. Thenceforward it was pursued vigorously, and culminated in 1893, when the Government pronounced in favour of adult suffrage. But the difficulties were not at an end: the Bill of that year was wrecked, mainly because its adoption was to be dependent upon an affirmative plebiscite; reintroduced in the following year without the obnoxious clause, it was passed through both Houses of Parliament, though only by the bare statutory majority in the Assembly, and shortly afterwards received the Queen's assent.

During the course of the debates the Premier, who holds the portfolio of Attorney-General, said that, if women were entitled to vote, they would have the right to sit in Parliament, and the Assembly, by twenty-eight votes to eight, refused to exclude them. A doubt has since been expressed, which is not shared by the Ministry, whether they are qualified to be elected to the Council. I have not had the opportunity to read the arguments, which concern the interpretation of several statutes, but they would be of no great interest, the main point being that Parliament intended to enable women to sit in both Houses.

In New Zealand, on the other hand, the enfranchising Act of 1893 expressly denied to women the right of election to the House of Representatives or nomination to the Council; and the succeeding House, though elected under adult suffrage, refused to go back upon this decision. The subsequent proposal of the Premier that women should be eligible for nomination to the Council, was intended, I believe, partly as a bid for their support, partly as a means of casting ridicule upon the non-representative body.

The first elections in South Australia under the new franchise were held early in 1896, and, apart from a few rural constituencies in which the issues were personal rather than political, were contested under three recognised programmes. The National Defence League, or Opposition, mentioned in its programme no items which were likely to be especially attractive to the female voters, and treated as open questions temperance legislation, and religious instruction in State' schools; the Labour platform, with discreet vagueness, advocated any equitable and reasonable claims of women for the amendment of the laws; and the Ministerial policy, as enunciated by the Premier, included an amendment of the Licensed Victuallers' Act in the direction of greater local control over licenses, and various measures of social reform, of which the principal were the raising of the age of consent, the simplification of the remedies of deserted wives, and the restriction of the importation and sale of opium. It should be mentioned, however, that, as the Labour Party are united in a close, though independent, alliance with the Government, the supporters of the one in many cases voted for the candidates of the other. In several constituencies a Ministerialist and a Labour man contested the two seats and received jointly the assistance of both parties.

As the Women's Franchise League had been dissolved upon the attainment of its purpose, the only organisation which interested itself, specifically, in the female voters was the W.C.T.U., which, having drawn up a scheme of reforms, suggested that it should be used as a basis for ascertaining the views of candidates, but did not seek directly to influence the votes of its members though leaning, undoubtedly, to the side of the Government. Its efforts to instruct women in the method of voting enabled returning officers to congratulate them on their knowledge of the business. From personal observation I can bear witness to the extreme orderliness of the proceedings, both during and after the poll.

The elections resulted in a slight accession of strength to the ranks of the Ministerialists and Labour members. As these are very Radical, the majority of women, contrary to the expectations of many, had failed to display Conservative predilections. It would seem, indeed, if we take also

into consideration the result of two General Elections in New Zealand, that their so-called Conservatism takes the form, not of an aversion from
advanced legislation, but of a disinclination to bring
about a change of Ministry.   Under masculine
influences, South Australia had forty-two Ministries
in forty years ; women entered the arena and a
Ministry which had held office for three years was
again returned to power.   An allowance must, of
course, be made for a feeling of gratitude to those
through whom the privilege of the vote had been
obtained.   Equally wrong was the anticipation that
the women would be found to be subject to clerical influences.   At the instigation of those who were under
this impression, the electors were invited, under a
direct reference, to say whether they desired the
introduction of religious instruction in State schools
during school hours and the payment of a capitation grant to denominational schools for secular
results.   Both questions were answered emphati-
cally in the negative, the second by a majority of
more than three votes to one.   The W.C.T.U. was
in favour of religious instruction, but strongly
opposed to the capitation grant.

The general conclusion formed after the elections
was that, in the vast majority of cases, the women
had voted in the same way as their masculine
relatives, and that domestic harmony had not been
disturbed.   It was impossible to obtain definite data,
as the Premier refused, rightly enough, to sanction

the issue of different voting papers for the two sexes. But, even if the female franchise merely increased the number of votes and did not affect the result of the elections, it does not follow that it has been nugatory.

Members who have to consider the wishes of female as well as male constituents will shape their actions accordingly. The effects of this influence cannot yet be studied fully in South Australia, as they were not manifested, to any great extent, in the first session of the new Parliament. A Licensed Victuallers' Act was passed, as had been promised by the Premier, which instituted local control over the issue of licenses, but provided, in accordance with statutory enactment, that the refusal of licenses, or reduction in their number, should be accompanied by compensation to the parties directly interested. As the Province has a steadily growing industry in the cultivation of the vine, Prohibitionists will be met by a serious obstacle to their crusade. In pursuance of an *ad feminas captandas* agitation for the prohibition of the employment of barmaids which had been carried on during the elections, the Assembly inserted a clause in the Bill which prohibited their employment after a certain number of years, but submitted to its excision by the Council. A Bill which would have given to widows a legal right to one-third of their deceased husband's property was discussed, but allowed to lapse. The Franchise Act, I should have stated, allowed a female elector, upon the completion of certain formalities, to vote through the post if she would be absent from her home on the day of the election, a privilege already accorded to men, or if she were resident more than three miles from the nearest polling place, or, by reason of the state of her health, would probably be unable to vote at the polling place on the day of the poll. This provision, which permitted open voting, was found to have led to abuses, and the Government passed an amending Act which withdrew all the supplementary privileges except the last, and required absent voters to fill in the paper at a postmaster's office and without supervision. As I was not in South Australia during the session, I am unable to give more than a brief summary of the proceedings which may be connected, directly or indirectly, with the extension of the franchise to women.

But when we turn to New Zealand, where a House elected under adult suffrage has fulfilled its allotted term of three years, we may expect to find more definite results. In that Province, as in South Australia, women were enfranchised by a House which had received no popular mandate to that effect ; in fact, the matter had scarcely been discussed in the constituencies, though attention had been drawn to it by the advocacy of several successive Premiers. In 1892, however, a new Electoral Bill, which conferred the franchise on all adult women, was passed by the House of Representatives

and accepted by the Council subject to the insertion
of a clause which absolved women in some cases
from attendance at the polling booth. The Government refused to accept the amendment, and the Bill
lapsed for the session. In the following year it was
reintroduced in the original form, and was passed
by both Houses, though only by a slender majority
in the Council. The Act contains the striking and,
as far as I know, unique provision that the names of
voters who have not exercised their privileges are
to be erased from the rolls, though a claim for
reinstatement may be made at the next periodical
revision.

The elections, which took place at the end of
1893, aroused widespread interest in the members
of the fair sex, of whom nine out of every eleven
who were registered went to the poll and proved
conclusively that, though the desire for the vote
might not have been general, women would not
refrain from its exercise. With the help of their
lords and masters, they falsified the expectations of
those who had anticipated a reaction in favour of Conservatism, by retaining in power, with an increased
majority, a Government which is, in some respects,
even more Radical than that of South Australia.
So complete was the defeat of the Opposition that it
was reduced to a remnant of twenty members in a
House of seventy-four. Another important feature
was the return of a body of Prohibitionists who
aimed at legislation which would enable the electors

in a locality to close all the public-houses by a bare majority. As they sat on both sides of the House, they did not affect the numerical strength of the two parties, but constituted a force which it was impossible for the Government to ignore. But while the consequent liquor legislation and the increased prominence of the temperance movement are the principal effects of the extension of the franchise to women, other measures of considerable importance are connected with the new factor in the sphere of politics.

Some of these would, doubtless, have been passed in any case. The Shops and Shop Assistants Act of 1894, for instance, which limits the total number of hours in a week, and the number of consecutive hours in a day, during which women and persons under eighteen years of age may be employed in a shop, and requires shopkeepers to provide sitting accommodation for their female employés, was passed by the preceding House of Representatives, and would have become law but for its rejection by the Council. Similarly, the greater stringency in the limitation of the hours of employment of women and young persons in factories, the exclusion of young persons from certain dangerous trades, and the prohibition of the employment of women within a month of their confinement, all of which were included in the Factories Act of the same year, might have been expected in the natural progress of industrial legislation. The appointment of women, also, as inspectors of factories, gaols, and asylums is in accordance with the recent practice of other countries. The same may be said of the Infant Life Protection Act, which seeks to prevent baby-farming, and of Acts dealing with the adoption of children and with industrial schools, though it is probable that their passage has been hastened by a knowledge of the approval of the female voters. Their influence is also seen in measures such as the raising of the age of consent to sixteen, in a country, be it remembered, in which girls come much more early to maturity than in England, the permission accorded to women to be enrolled as barristers and solicitors, and the simplification of the procedure where a judicial separation is desired. Parliament has discussed, but without legislative results, proposals that the sexes should be placed on an equality as regards the grounds for a divorce, and that a divorce should be obtainable if either party become insane or be sentenced to a long term of imprisonment.

But we can trace the influence of women most directly in the desire of the Premier, to which I have referred, to render them eligible for nomination to the Council, and in the attempts to put an end to the legal sanction accorded by the State to betting, immorality, and drink. In these matters members are face to face with the most pronounced opinions of their female constituents.

The prevention of gambling is sought through the

suppression of the totalisator, which was legalised
in 1889. In the following years, it is admitted, the
number of licenses issued was in excess of the
requirements of the population, and it was felt, even
by the advocates of the machine, when a strongly
supported effort was made in the House of Representatives to abolish it, that a concession was
inevitable. In its final form the measure reduced
by one-third the number of licenses which might
be issued thenceforward, and prohibited all persons
from betting with minors and from laying or taking
odds dependent upon the dividend paid by the
totalisator.

The female voters are even more anxious to secure
the repeal of the C.D. Act, though it has for several
years been a dead letter. It only applies to districts
which the Government declares to be subject to its
provisions, and no Ministry at the present time
would venture to recommend its application nor
Municipal Council to proffer such a request. But
the women will not be satisfied until they have
expunged from the Statute Book an Act which they
declare to be a disgrace to New Zealand. Their
purpose would have been effected by a short
measure which was passed by the House of Representatives but rejected by the nominated Legislative
Council, which is less amenable to public opinion.
They have also inspired the Government to greater
stringency in the administration of the law against
keepers of houses of ill-fame, which has led, accord-

ing to common report, to a large increase in the prevalence of venereal diseases.

In order to understand the position of affairs as it affects the Prohibitionists in their crusade against public-houses, it is necessary to have some knowledge, in their broadest aspects, of the constitution and powers of the licensing authority and of the gradual extension of popular control. Under an Act of 1881 the regulation of the traffic was placed in the hands of elective Licensing Committees, and the first step in the direction of popular control was taken by the provision that additional licenses, except in special cases, should not be granted until they had been demanded by a poll of the ratepayers. Objections to the granting or renewal of licenses might be made by private individuals, the police and corporate bodies, and should specify, as the ground of objection, that the proposed licensee was an undesirable person, that the premises were unsuitable, or that "the licensing thereof is not required in the neighbourhood." The words that I have quoted were seized upon by the Prohibitionists, who had gathered strength during the following years as a justification for the refusal of all licenses if they could capture the Licensing Committee. In Sydenham, a suburb of Christchurch, they were at length successful, and were confronted with the bitter antagonism of the brewers. After several years of litigation they were defeated conclusively, and were thrown back upon an agitation for the amendment of the law.

The next important measure, that of 1893, was passed by representatives elected under manhood suffrage, who knew that when they sought a renewal of confidence they would be called upon to justify their actions, not only in the eyes of Prohibitionists, but in those of the newly enfranchised female electors. We shall therefore not be surprised to find that the Act introduced a great extension of the principle of popular control. It placed both the election of the Licensing Committees and the Local Option polls on the basis of adult suffrage and enlarged the scope of the latter. Previously, as we have seen, the electors were only allowed to decide' as to the advisability of additional licenses. Herein their power was curtailed, as such polls were not to be held unless a census had shown that the population of a district had increased by 25 per cent. in the quinquennial period. This was a concession to Prohibitionists who would welcome a change which rendered the increase of licenses more difficult. But the principal innovation was the control given to the electorate over the renewal of all publicans' accommodation or bottle licenses. Triennial polls were to be held, at which they were to be invited to say whether they desired the continuation, reduction, or abolition of licenses, subject to the proviso that prohibition would not be deemed to be carried except by a three-fifths majority of the votes, and that the poll would be void unless it had been attended by a majority of the registered electors.

Should prohibition not be carried, the votes in its favour were to be added to those cast for reduction, and, in the event of reduction, the Licensing Committee were to refuse to renew the licences of not more than one in four of the publicans in the district, commencing with those whose licenses had been endorsed, and proceeding with those who offered little or no accommodation to travellers. No provision was made for compensation to persons who, through no fault of their own, might be dispossessed of their licenses. As the Act declared that the poll should be regarded as void unless one-half of the electors recorded their votes, it was to the obvious interest of anti-prohibitionists to abstain from attendance at the booths, and the figures consequently afford no index of the full strength of the opposing parties. The Prohibitionists, however, had little cause to be dissatisfied with the results of their first appeal to the electorate, which included women as well as men : prohibition was carried in one case, reduction in fourteen, while in the remainder the poll was either void or the votes were cast in favour of existing conditions.

The amending Act of 1895 has made no substantial alterations in the law in spite of the persistent agitation of Prohibitionists in favour of prohibition on the vote of a bare majority. It was decreed that licensing polls should be held concurrently with General Elections, that voters should

be allowed to vote both for prohibition and reduction, though the two votes could, naturally, no
longer be combined in favour of the latter, that
the vote should affect all forms of licenses, and,
in view of the district in which prohibition had
been carried, that, in such cases, the issue should
be between the continued refusal of licenses and
their restoration to the former number. Under the
present law, it will be noted, should successive
reductions lead to the cancellation of all licenses,
a vote of the electors can never restore more licenses
than existed at the time when the last was doomed
to extinction.

The second poll was taken at the end of 1896 and
resulted in the failure to carry either prohibition or
reduction in any district. The figures were as
follows : continuation, 139,249 ; reduction, 94,226 ;
prohibition, 98,103. Though the Prohibitionists had
been enabled to increase their vote by nearly 50,000
and had therein sufficient grounds for the hope of
ultimate success, it is probable that they would have
been more successful but for the intemperance of
their leaders, who aim at prohibition alone and care
neither for the regulation of the traffic nor for reduction. They were also handicapped by the frantic
efforts of the brewers, who spent their ample funds
freely and were able to command the votes of many
who were interested, either directly or indirectly, in
the trade ; and by an alliance between the brewers
and many of the Ministerialists. While the General

Election and the Local Option poll constituted distinct issues, and there was no reason why a supporter of the Government should feel bound to vote for the continuation of licenses, it is an un-doubted fact that a large number of the women of the working classes, who might have been expected to be opposed to the public-houses, voted, on that occasion, in favour of their retention. At Wellington, where, as at Adelaide, I was struck by the prevailing orderliness, the only women whom I noted as taking an active part in the proceedings were canvassing in favour of the brewers.

At first sight it seems strange that the brewers should have worked with the party which had passed the most stringent liquor legislation on the Statute Book, but it must be remembered that this question had neither been debated nor divided the House on the ordinary lines of cleavage. The brewers, many persons maintain, know that they have the sympathy of the Government which, according to this hypothesis, has done as little as possible to meet the wishes of the Prohibitionists, and that only under virtual compulsion, and, in its measure of 1896, introduced a Bill which would certainly be rejected by the Council and was cal-culated to cast ridicule upon the agitation of the Prohibitionists. It was provided therein that a fourth issue should be added at the Local Option polls, that of national prohibition, and that, if it were carried by a three-fifths majority of the votes recorded in all the districts, it should be unlawful, subject to the exception mentioned hereafter, to import into the Province any liquor for any purpose or to distil it in the Province or to manufacture it for sale or barter. No person selling any spirituous or distilled perfume, nor any apothecary, chemist, or druggist administering or selling any spirituous, distilled, or fermented liquor for medicinal use, should do so otherwise than in such combination as rendered it unfit for use as a beverage. The Governor might declare, by notice in *The Gazette*, by what combination of ingredients the articles would be rendered sufficiently unpalatable. Persons requiring liquor for medicinal use or use in the arts and manufacturers were to make applications to Her Majesty's Customs and if their *bonâ fides* were proved, might receive it, for ready money, "in such closed and sealed bottles or other receptacle as that the liquor therein cannot be poured out without such seal being first broken," and attached "with a Government label declaring the kind, quantity, quality, and price of the liquor, as these may be determined by the Governor." In this measure the Government seem to have attempted to run with the hare and hunt with the hounds. The brewers would laugh in their sleeves and the Prohibitionists would welcome a measure which instituted machinery for the attainment of national prohibition. If the assumption be correct, the latter are credited with a lamentable lack of any sense of humour ; from all

appearances they are not prepared to allow themselves to be hoodwinked.

Many of the representatives seem to have had an
equally low opinion of the average intelligence of
female electors, as they sought to capture the votes
of domestic servants by a Bill which was rejected
by the Council, in which a weekly half-holiday was
decreed to them except in cases of sickness or death
in the family, or where an annual holiday of not less
than fourteen days had been substituted by mutual
agreement between employers and their servants.
How the period of rest was to be enforced was,
perhaps wisely, not laid down, as domestics would,
in few cases, be prepared to give information against
their employers. Those among the latter, however,
who took the matter seriously would, presumably,
guard themselves against judiciary proceedings by
compelling their servants to be out of the house on
the holiday between three o'clock and half-past nine,
whatever might be the state of the weather. Again,
the undoubted evil, that young girls, by the culpable
weakness of their parents, are allowed to parade the
streets at night, was to be cured, according to the
Government, by the so-called Juvenile Depravity
Suppression Bill, which failed to meet with acceptance by the usually docile House of Representatives.
Its danger and absurdity can be gathered, without
further comment, from the quotation of one of the
clauses : "Whenever any constable finds any girl"
(who is apparently not over the age of sixteen years)

"loitering in the streets or in out-of-the-way places after the hour of ten of the clock at night, and he has reason to believe that she is there for improper purposes, the following provisions shall apply :—

"1. He shall forthwith take her to the nearest beat of another constable, or, failing him, to the nearest justice or clergyman, or, failing him, to the nearest house of some married person of good repute, in whose presence the girl shall be questioned as to her name, her abode, her parents or guardians, and her reason for being from home and loitering as aforesaid.

"2. The constable shall then take, or shall cause her to be taken, to her home, where she shall be handed over to the person in charge of the house, and the constable shall forthwith on his return from duty make report of the facts to the officer in charge of the station."

Should the offence be repeated and the girl's reply be deemed by the officer in charge of a police station to be unsatisfactory, she may be brought before a magistrate and be committed to a reformatory or an industrial school. Some justification, I must add, for the seemingly depreciatory opinion of the members was afforded by the proceedings at the convention of the National Council of Women held at Christchurch early in 1896. This Association, which claims to be non-political and to focus the views of the women of New Zealand, passed reso-

lutions in favour of the nationalisation of the land,
a compulsory eight hours' day, and the enactment
of a minimum rate of wages ; but the climax was
reached when it was resolved that "in all cases
where a woman elects to superintend her own
household and to be the mother of children, there
shall be a law attaching a certain just share of her
husband's earnings or income for her separate use,
payable if she so desires it into her separate account." The first portion of this sentence is mys-
terious, and seems to be based on the assumption
that the husband has nothing to say in the matter.

The extraordinary legislative activity which I have
summarised need arouse no astonishment, as it is in
consonance with the usual practice of the Parliament
of New Zealand. Between the years 1876 and 1894,
it has been computed, 2,972 measures were passed,
and of these no less than 1,602 have already been
repealed.

So much for the past : we must now consider
briefly the present position of affairs and the further
effects which may be anticipated from female
suffrage.

It is the general impression that while a large
majority of the women voted in 1893 as their
husbands and brothers advised them, yet they
were induced, in many instances, by their leagues,
which had been started on independent lines, to
support candidates on moral rather than political
considerations. In the following year these leagues,

with the exception of those which placed liquor
questions before all others, were captured by one
of the political parties, most of them by the
Ministerialists. An amusing incident occurred in
this connection at Dunedin. Shortly before the
last elections it was decided, at a thinly-attended
meeting of the Women's Franchise League, to
support the three Ministerial candidates, although
one of them was an anti-prohibitionist. Thereupon
many of the members protested against the party
character given to the association, and called a
meeting, the proceedings at which were thus
described by the local newspaper :—

" The meeting which was held yesterday afternoon
in connection with the Women's Franchise League
was, in some respects, the most unique gathering
ever held in the city. There were nearly 200
women present, and they were divided into two
parties—the followers of Mrs. Hatton and the
supporters of Mrs. Don and Mrs. Hislop. At the
close of the opening remarks of the Chairman (the
Rev. Mr. Saunders), Mr. Hatton mounted the platform, and declining to take his seat, the Chairman
threatened to send for a policeman. Then occurred
a scene and uproar, of which it is impossible to give
any conception. The noise was deafening, and
attracted to the spot passers-by in the street.
Half a dozen persons occupied the stage, and
while some persons were addressing the meeting,
others were engaged in heated argument. Women

stamped on the floor with their feet and parasols,
others were speaking at the highest pitch of their
voices; there were hissing and hooting, and other
unwomanly demonstrations. Eventually a portion
of Mrs. Hislop's supporters withdrew to a side
room, and the Chairman, having dissolved the
meeting, vacated the chair." [1]

We find, therefore, that, with the exception of
ardent Prohibitionists, women are subordinating
their special interests to their increasing attachment
to one or other of the parties; but it does not follow
that they will cease to exercise a direct influence
upon legislation. It is not easy to learn to what
extent their views have been modified during the
last few years. The proceedings of the National
Council of Women cannot be taken seriously, and
the practical aspirations of the sex must be sought
rather in the points emphasised by the local leagues.
The files of the newspapers, unfortunately, afford
little information, as it was the practise of candidates
to speak upon general topics at their public meetings,
and to take part in informal and unreported discussions with the members of the various women's
leagues. On these occasions, I understand, and I
must again except the Prohibitionists, the women
made their views known, but did not seek to exact
pledges as a condition of support. It is believed
that they took less interest in the second elections,
but statistics are not yet available for a comparison

---

[1] *Otago Daily Times*, November 2, 1896.

of the numbers that went to the poll on the two occasions. Of 9,332 women who were registered for the City of Auckland, 6,304 recorded their votes, but I am unable to say whether the proportion of about seven in ten holds good for the Province.

But, while it is necessary to consider the view of local leagues in order to form general conclusions as to the trend of female thought, it is found that, in the absence of one predominating centre, different issues obtain prominence in different places, and that the vote lacks the force which would be given to it by concentration. A general similarity of aims, however, enables an estimate to be formed of the questions which the women will press upon the attention of Parliament in the immediate future. The repeal of the C.D. and Totalisator Acts, amendments of the marriage laws, and greater protection of women and children against the cruelty of husbands and fathers, are subjects which are certain again to provoke discussion. Parliament will also be asked again to admit women within its precincts, as they are no longer satisfied with the possession of the franchise; but the agitation will, I think, at present be unsuccessful, partly because, in the only instance in which a woman has held a public position, the experiment is regarded as having been a failure. Some three years ago Mrs. Yates was elected to be Mayor of Onehunga, and was unable to fill the position satisfactorily. She was a woman of considerable ability, but of a hasty temper, and came into constant conflict with the Councillors. Very possibly they did not give her a fair chance; but the fact remains that the proceedings excited much ridicule, in the press and elsewhere, and retarded the movement in favour of rendering women eligible for seats in Parliament.

The Prohibitionists do not count upon much legislative assistance during the next three years, as the number of members of the House of Representatives who are in favour of prohibition upon the vote of a bare majority was reduced by the last election. They believe that if the "National Option" Bill be re-introduced, the Council may seize upon that fact as a ground for again rejecting it. In the meanwhile, they will concentrate their efforts upon the education of the electorate, and have, as I have shown, no reason to be discouraged by the results of the second local option poll.

"Equal wages for equal work" is a new cry of the female voters. They believe that if the Government were to introduce the principle of equal wages for similar work as between the men and women in the Civil Service, private employers would gradually follow the example. This proposal has the support both of those who desire to raise the wages of women and of those who think that they would no longer be able to compete with men in the search for employment. It might have been expected that the habit which women have now acquired of meeting together for the discussion of a common policy would have inclined them to the formation of Trades Unions; but it is too early to look for indirect results from female suffrage, which has hitherto had no appreciable effect upon the rate of wages of women. Nor has it modified the domestic instincts of the vast majority of the sex.

Lastly, the women of the working classes, almost without exception, are in favour of pensions to the aged and needy, and regard objections based on the deterrence of thrift or the difficulty of raising the necessary funds as factitious and disingenuous. Herein, as in some of the other matters to which I have referred, we see the principal danger of female suffrage in New Zealand, the tendency of the women to subordinate reason to sentiment. They note the prevalence of an evil, and believe that if the State decrees its cessation it will promptly cease to exist. But we must cherish the hope, though the justification for it is not yet manifest, that as the women become accustomed to the exercise of their power, they will no longer take a purely emotional view of the problems which engage their attention. At the same time, as we have seen, they have promoted several unobtrusive but eminently useful reforms which would have had less chance of acceptance in a House elected by men. It is in this direction, and not in attempts to make people virtuous or sober by Act of Parliament, that we may anticipate the best results from the enfranchisement of the women of New Zealand.

IX

THE EVOLUTION OF A FEDERAL GOVERNMENT

THE five self-governing Provinces of the mainland of Australia have been evolved from the Crown Colonies of New South Wales, South Australia, and Western Australia by the successive detachment of Victoria and Queensland from the former and the gradual growth of the system of responsible government, and are separated by lines of demarcation which, except where the Murray or one of its tributaries forms the boundary, are purely arbitrary and have not been drawn in accordance with any distinctive geographical features. In the exercise of fiscal autonomy as regards their reciprocal relations, they have adopted protective tariffs which have not only impeded the interchange of commodities, but in some cases diverted trade from its natural course. New South Wales, indeed, after a period of protection, has reverted to the policy of free trade, while the tariffs of Queensland and Western Australia are directed mainly to the

acquisition of revenue ; but they are actually protective, as are, avowedly and to a high degree,
those of Victoria and South Australia. Under
these circumstances, and as the result of insufficient intercourse, antagonistic interests have been
created and jealousies aroused which are a source
of anxiety to those who consider the future of
Australia.

The dangers which would be likely to arise from
the independent development of the Provinces were
recognised at an early date. At the time of the
suggested separation of the district of Port Phillip
from New South Wales and of the discussion of the
new constitutions which were about to be granted,
it was proposed by the Imperial Authorities that the
government should be in the hands of a General
Assembly and local Provincial Councils, but it was
objected by the colonists that, in the absence of
regular means of communication, any scheme which
included the creation of a central legislature and
executive would be found to be impracticable. In
deference to their views the idea was allowed to
drop, and no attempt was made to secure unity of
action between the Provinces, except that, in 1850,
the Governor of New South Wales received a commission as Governor - General of Australia and
Governor of Victoria, South Australia and Tasmania,
the administrators of which obtained the rank of
Lieutenant-Governor. They were to be superseded
in their authority by the former when he was in

their territories, but were instructed to correspond directly with the Colonial Office. It is not clear to what extent the Governor-General was expected to direct the administration of the other Provinces. Some writers maintain that his pre-eminence was purely titular and intended as a compliment to the Mother Colony. In any case, when, a few years later, responsible government was established and the Governors gradually became little more than figure-heads of the Executive, the matter ceased to be of any importance.

The next phase in the movement originated in Victoria upon the initiative of Mr. (now Sir Charles) Gavan Duffy, who, in 1857, induced the Legislative Assembly to appoint a committee to consider the advisability of federal union. Upon their recommendation that an inter-provincial conference should be held, communications were addressed to New South Wales, South Australia, and Tasmania, which, though separated from the mainland of Australia, has always identified itself closely with Australian affairs. The proposal was in each case favourably received, as also, a little later, by Queensland, which had been erected into a separate Province in 1859 ; and Tasmania actually appointed its delegates. But there the matter was allowed to rest ; and, although occasional conferences were held at which a uniform tariff, the immigration of the Chinese, and other subjects were discussed, no practical steps were taken until 1883, when external questions impressed

Australian statesmen with the necessity for the
creation of some body which would voice the
opinions of Australia. Germany was reputed to
have designs upon New Guinea, France upon the
New Hebrides; while the latter country also gave
offence by the penal settlement in New Caledonia.
In the spring of that year Sir T. M'Ilwraith, the
Premier of Queensland, which from its position has
the greatest interest in New Guinea, had hoisted the
British flag on the Island and taken formal possession of that part of it which was not under the
control of the Dutch ; but his action had been dis-
avowed by the Imperial Government. A convention,
attended by representatives from the five Australian
Provinces, Tasmania, New Zealand, and Fiji, was
accordingly held at Sydney, at which a decision was
arrived at as to the main principles which were
embodied in the Federal Council Act of 1885, the
first legislative recognition of the Unity of Australia.
Under this Act it was provided that a Federal
Council, containing two representatives from a self-
governing Province and one from a Crown Colony,
should come into existence as soon as four of the
Australasian Provinces had expressed their willingness to join it, and should thenceforward hold
biennial sessions. The motive which had called
the Council into existence was shown clearly in the
principal power delegated to it, that of legislating,
subject to Imperial approval, in regard to the
relations of Australasia with the Islands of the

Pacific. It was also authorised to deal, among other subjects, with the fisheries in Australasian waters beyond territorial limits and certain aspects of civil and criminal jurisdiction, upon which it could pass enactments which would bind the Provinces represented upon it; and with questions such as general defences, quarantine, copyright, uniformity of weights and measures, and others which might be referred to it by the Legislatures of two or more Provinces, and any other matters of general Australasian interest on which the Legislatures can legislate within their own limits, but as to which it is deemed desirable that there should be a law of general application. Such legislation, however, was to take effect only in the Provinces that requested the Council to act, and in any others that might subsequently adopt it. It will thus be seen that the measure is of a purely permissive character, as each Province decides for itself whether it will be represented on the Council. New South Wales, mainly under the influence of the late Sir Henry Parkes, and New Zealand have never taken part in the deliberations, and South Australia has only been represented on a single occasion. The abstention of New Zealand is of smaller importance, from her geographical position and her intention not to identify herself at present with any scheme of Australian federation; but the hostility of New South Wales and the apathy of South Australia have placed great obstacles in the way of Queensland, Victoria, Western Australia, and Tasmania, which, and especially Victoria, have attempted to turn the Council to the best account. Other causes have combined to minimise its utility; it has neither an Executive to carry out, nor a judiciary to enforce its decisions ; it has no control over public funds ; and, as has recently been pointed out, "it transacts its business without a Ministry or a department, without a leader or an Opposition, without a party or a programme; there is no necessary continuity of representation, or similarity in the mode of appointment of representatives, or fixed area within which its legislation has force ; it is vagrant in domicile and without a roof to shelter it, without a foot of territory to rest upon, without a ship or a soldier to protect it, without a single man in its service, or a shilling of its own to pay one."[1] But, in spite of these drawbacks, the Council has done practical work : it has paved the way for a system of national defence by the establishment of federal garrisons at King George's Sound and Thursday Island ; it has regulated the pearl-shell and bêche-de-mer fisheries on the coasts of Queensland and Western Australia, and it has interested itself actively in the promotion of the proposed Pacific cable. More would have been done, particularly in the consideration of the matters referred to it by Provincial Legislatures, had

[1] "The Federal Council of Australasia," by the Hon. Alfred Deakin, *Australasian Review of Reviews*, February, 1895.

it not been hoped that by the postponement of
action the Council would be enabled, through the
adhesion of South Australia and New South Wales,
to legislate for the whole of Australia. Several of
the Provinces, notably Western Australia and .
Queensland, which have shown little eagerness for
the immediate realisation of a closer union, believed
that the Council would, by a gradual process of
development, be transformed into a Federal Parliament, and were prepared to allow events to take
their natural course ; but in other quarters a strong
feeling arose, which was strengthened by the report
of Imperial officers on the condition of the Provincial Defences, that the time had arrived when an
attempt should be made to draft a Federal Constitution Bill which should be submitted to the
various Provinces, and, if approved by them, to the
Imperial. Authorities. As the result of correspondence between the Premiers, delegates from the whole
of Australasia, with the exception of Fiji, met at
Melbourne in 1890, and passed resolutions which
led to the convocation at Sydney in the following year of a constituent convention, which was
attended by Parliamentary representatives from
the seven Provinces. The convention sat for
several weeks, under the presidency of Sir Henry
Parkes, and drew up a Bill "to constitute the
commonwealth of Australia," which formed the
basis of the discussions at the recent Federal
Convention.

The legislative powers of the Commonwealth are, under the provisions of the Bill, vested in a Governor - General, appointed by the Queen, a Senate, and a House of Representatives. The laws passed by the Parliament are to be presented to the Governor-General, who may assent to them in the Queen's name, reserve them for the signification of her pleasure, withhold his assent, or return them to the Parliament with any amendments that he may recommend. Laws assented to by the Governor-General may be disallowed within two years by the Queen in Council, and laws that have been reserved shall not come into force unless within the same period they have received the assent of the Queen in Council. The Members of the Convention did not deem it necessary that any class of Bills should be reserved, but understood that, as they proposed that the Commonwealth should be able to legislate on several matters affecting the relations of Australia with foreign nations, the Constitution would not be acceptable to the Imperial Authorities unless a considerable power of intervention were reserved to them.

The Senate is to be composed of eight members for each Province, which is henceforth to be called a State, of whom one-half retire triennially, directly chosen by the Houses of Parliament of the several States for a period of six years. Senators are subject to no property qualification, but must be of

the age of thirty years, have resided for five years
within the limits of the Commonwealth, be entitled
to vote for a member of the House of Representatives, and if not British subjects by birth, have
been naturalised for at least five years before the
time of their election. Bankrupts, criminals, and
Government contractors are specially disqualified.
Similar provisions and disqualifications apply to
members of the House of Representatives, except
that the minimum age is reduced to twenty-one
years, and that the periods of residence and
naturalisation are reduced from five years to
three. They are to be chosen, in constituencies
of thirty thousand inhabitants, by electors whose
qualification shall be that prescribed by each
State as the qualification for electors of its more
numerous House of Parliament. The members of
both Houses are to be paid at the rate of £500 a
year, and are precluded from sitting in a State
Parliament. The Parliament of the Commonwealth is to have authority to deal with "external
affairs and treaties," to take over the powers of
the Federal Council, which will cease to exist from
the date of its establishment, and to have the exclusive right to legislate in regard to the affairs
of the people of any race, not being Australian
aboriginals or Maoris of New Zealand, with respect
to whom it is deemed desirable to make laws not
applicable to the general community; the seat of
the Federal Government and any places required

for Federal purposes ; and the provisional administration of any territory surrendered by any State,
and accepted by the Commonwealth, or any territory in the Pacific placed by the Queen under the
authority of and accepted by the Commonwealth.
The framers of the Constitution doubtless had in
view the Northern Territory, which, as it forms a
heavy burden upon its resources, South Australia
might be glad to hand over to the Federation.
The Federal Parliament is also to deal exclusively
with the postal and telegraphic services, military
and naval defences and munitions of war, ocean
beacons and lighthouses, quarantine, and, as soon
as a uniform tariff has been imposed, with foreign
and internal trade, bounties and duties of customs
and excise. In the meanwhile, the duties are to be
collected by Federal officials, but will be those that
are, or may be, imposed by the Parliaments of the
several States. Upon the enactment of a uniform
Federal tariff, all such State laws will thereby be
repealed and "trade and intercourse throughout
the Commonwealth, whether by means of internal
carriage or ocean navigation, shall be absolutely
free." The expenditure of the Commonwealth is
to be charged to the several States in proportion
to the numbers of their people, and any surplus of
revenue over expenditure is to be returned to them
in proportion to the amount of revenue raised
therein respectively, subject to certain reservations
and to the right of the Federal Parliament, after

the imposition of a uniform tariff, to prescribe the method of its disposal. The Federal revenue is to consist of customs and excise duties and of moneys raised by any other mode or system of taxation, but so that all such taxation shall be uniform through the Commonwealth. The Federal Parliament may also, " with the consent of the Parliaments of all the States, make laws for taking over and consolidating the whole or any part of the public debt of any State or States ; but so that a State shall be liable to indemnify the Commonwealth in respect of the amount of a debt taken over, and that the amount of interest payable in respect of a debt shall be deducted and retained from time to time from the share of the surplus revenue of the Commonwealth which would be otherwise payable to the State." [1] Certain other legislative powers are vested in the Federal Parliament, which may concurrently be exercised by the several States, and in such cases Federal shall supersede State legislation. All subjects not exclusively vested in the Parliament of the Commonwealth, or withdrawn from the Parliaments of the several States, are reserved to, and shall remain vested in, the State Parliaments.

The authority of the Senate in regard to Money Bills formed the subject of much discussion, and was decided by a compromise which, it was hoped, would satisfy both those who desired to secure the

[1] Cap. iv., Clause 13.

financial supremacy of the House of Representatives and the inhabitants of the smaller States, who would naturally struggle for the rights of the Senate in which they would be on a footing of equality with their more powerful neighbours. The views of the former were met by the provisions that "laws appropriating any part of the public revenue, or imposing any tax or impost, shall originate in the House of Representatives," and that "the Senate shall have equal power with the House of Representatives in respect to all proposed laws, except laws imposing taxation and laws appropriating the necessary supplies for the ordinary annual services of the Government, which the Senate may affirm or reject, but may not amend. But the Senate may not amend any proposed law in such a manner as to increase any proposed charge or burden on the people." The interests of the latter were safeguarded by the four succeeding sub-sections :

"Laws imposing taxation shall deal with the imposition of taxation only.

"Laws imposing taxation, except laws imposing duties of customs on imports, shall deal with one subject of taxation only.

"The expenditure for services other than the ordinary annual services of the Government shall not be authorised by the same law as that which appropriates the supplies for such ordinary annual services, but shall be authorised by a separate law or laws.

" In the case of a proposed law which the Senate may not amend, the Senate may at any stage return it to the House of Representatives with a message requesting the omission or amendment of any items or provisions therein. And the House of Representatives may, if it thinks fit, make such omissions or amendments, or any of them, with or without modifications." [1]

The executive authority of the Commonwealth is to be exercised by the Governor-General as the Queen's representative, with the aid and advice of a Federal Executive Council. Considerable discussion took place at the Convention as to the relations which should exist between the Federal Executive and Legislature, some of the Representatives being in favour of the British system, others of the direct popular election of the head of the Government. It was finally agreed that the members of the Council should be chosen and summoned by the Governor-General, should hold office during his pleasure, and should be capable of being chosen and of sitting in either House of Parliament. They are to execute the provisions of the Constitution and the laws of the Commonwealth ; to assume at once control of the departments of customs and excise, posts and telegraphs, military and naval defence, ocean lights and quarantine ; and, until other provision is made by Parliament, to appoint and remove all other officers of the Government.

[1] Cap. i., Clauses 54 and 55.

The Parliament of the Commonwealth may establish a Supreme Court of Australia, consisting of a
Chief Justice and not less than four other Justices,
who shall be appointed by the Governor-General in
Council, and shall be irremovable except upon an
address from both Houses of Parliament. The
Supreme Court shall be a final Court of Appeal from
any other Federal Court, which may be established
by Parliament, and from the highest Court of final
resort in any State ; and may be invested by Parliament with final and conclusive jurisdiction in all
cases upon which an appeal has hitherto been
allowed to the Queen in Council, subject to the
right of the Queen to grant an appeal to herself in
Council against the judgment of the Supreme Court
in any case which concerns the public interests of
the Commonwealth, or of any State, or of any other
part of the British Empire. The Parliament may
also confer upon the Federal Courts, other than the
Supreme Court, jurisdiction to deal, either exclusively or concurrently with the Courts of the States,
with cases arising under the Constitution or under
any law made by the Parliament of the Commonwealth or affecting the Representatives of Foreign
Powers, and with certain other matters including
cases in which the Commonwealth is a party, or in
which a Writ of Mandamus or Prohibition is sought
against an officer of the Commonwealth.

As the powers of the State are to be substantially
those which they possess at present with the excep-

tion of such as are transferred to the Federal Legislature and Executive, it is only necessary to add that the Governors of the States are to be appointed in the manner which their Parliament may prescribe, but are to correspond with the Imperial Authorities through the Governor-General : that States are not to be subdivided nor deprived of any of their territories without the consent of their Parliaments ; and that they are forbidden explicitly to raise or maintain any military or naval force, to coin money, or make anything but gold and silver legal tender in payment of debts, to make any law prohibiting the free exercise of any religion, or to make or enforce any law abridging any privilege or immunity of citizens of other States of the Commonwealth, or to deny to any person within their jurisdiction the equal protection of the laws.

Finally, it is provided that any of the existing Provinces that have not adopted the Constitution may, upon doing so, be admitted to the Commonwealth, and that any law for the alteration of the Constitution is not to be submitted to the Governor-General for the Royal Assent until it has been passed by an absolute majority of both Houses of Parliament, and has been approved by conventions of a majority of the States representing a majority of the people of the Commonwealth.

When the Constitution Bill had been drafted, the next step should have been its reference to the Parliaments of the Constituent Provinces ; but it was

not even introduced in New South Wales, Queensland, Western Australia, or New Zealand. In
Victoria it was passed by the Assembly and forwarded
to the Council, which passed it subject to certain
amendments which were never considered by the
Assembly; in South Australia it was introduced in
the Assembly, and was dropped; in Tasmania it
passed the Assembly and was dropped at an early
stage in the Council. This procession of failures
caused the advocates of Federation to realise that
there must be something faulty in the method of
procedure, and to ask themselves whether it was
reasonable to expect that fourteen independent
Chambers, or twelve, if New Zealand be excluded,
should be able to arrive at a uniform decision on so
complicated and contentious a subject. It was felt,
also, that the Parliaments had no popular mandate
to deal with the question, and that, in the general
apathy and absence of interest, the electors themselves should be stirred up by direct participation in
the movement. Accordingly, Mr. Reid, the Premier
of New South Wales, invited the Premiers of the
other Australian Provinces to meet him at Hobart in
January, 1895, taking advantage of the fact that four
of them would be there in connection with the
biennial meeting of the Federal Council. The invi-
tation was accepted, and a new scheme was devised
of which the main principles were the popular election of delegates empowered to meet and frame a
Federal Constitution ; the reference of the Consti-

tution so framed to a plebiscite of the several electorates and its subsequent transmission for Imperial
legislation.   The Premiers of New South Wales,
Victoria, South Australia, and Tasmania accepted
the proposal in its entirety ; the Premier of Queensland agreed to it, except as regards the reference of
the Constitution to a plebiscite ; but the Premier of
Western Australia was unable to concur with the
decision of his colleagues.   Sir John Forrest did not
believe that popular election would lead to the
choice of the most highly trained jurists and finan-
ciers, who could alone frame a consistent and work-
able Constitution, and he regarded as absurd the
assumption that the average elector could give an
intelligent opinion upon a measure of so complicated
a character.   There is much force in these object
tions ; but it must be remembered that the former
effort failed from its dissociation from popular impulse, and that the delegates would have the benefit
of the work of their predecessors, which they would
be bound to accept as the basis of their deliberations.
As regards the plebiscite, it cannot have been expected that the vote of the bulk of the electorate
would be more than an affirmative or negative reply
upon the broadest issue ; but, assuming it to be
necessary that the Constitution Bill should in some
manner or other be submitted for the judgment of
each of the Provinces, the direct reference has the
merit of being expeditious and conclusive and of
avoiding the quagmire of Parliamentary discussions.

Before proceeding to note the results of the resolutions passed at the Premiers' Conference, it may
be of interest to consider to what extent recent
events have affected the status of the Federal
Council. As has already been remarked, it has pursued a policy of self-effacement, and in spite of the
increase in its numbers, it has never appealed to the
imagination of Australians. It was undoubtedly
dwarfed by comparison with the Federal Convention, which, indeed, decreed its contingent extinction, and it has, to some extent, been supplanted by
the informal meetings of Australian Premiers which
tend to become an annual institution. At a Conference held at Sydney in January, 1896, the urgent
necessity for Federation was again emphasised, and
it was resolved that, pending its attainment, the
military laws of the Provinces should be assimilated,
and a cordite factory be established under State
supervision. Resolutions were also passed in favour
of a Federal system of quarantine, the distribution
of the cost of lighthouses on the basis of population,
the extension to all coloured races of the provisions
of the Chinese Restriction Acts, and non-participa-
tion in the Anglo-Japanese Treaty. In this manner
the Premiers, instead of referring questions to the
Federal Council through their respective legislatures,
decided, after personal consultation, upon measures
which each would endeavour, in the common
interest, to pass through the Parliament of his own
Province. Other interprovincial conferences also

are becoming more common. The precautions to be adopted against the tick fever were discussed at Sydney in 1896, and a few months ago, earlier, several Ministers of Agriculture met the South Australian Minister at Adelaide and decided upon the advisability of uniform legislation which would promote similarity of out-put in the products of the different Provinces, such as frozen meat, butter, wine, and fruit, for which it was hoped to create a large market in England. It has been argued that the growing realisation of the interdependence of the Provinces and of the material advantages accruing from combined action, will tend to hasten the advent of Federation.

The new proposals in that direction were favourably received, and the Legislatures of New South Wales, Victoria, South Australia, and Tasmania passed the so-called Australasian Federation Enabling Act, in substantially similar form, upon the lines laid down by the Premiers. The details of their scheme may be gathered from the principal provisions of the Victorian Act :—

"The Convention shall consist of ten Representatives of each Colony represented.

"The Convention shall be charged with the duty of framing for Australasia a Federal Constitution under the Crown in the form of a Bill for enactment by the Imperial Parliament.

"Every Member and every person eligible for Membership of either House of Parliament shall be eligible for Membership of the Convention as a Representative of Victoria. And any one hundred or more electors duly qualified to vote for the election of a Member of the Legislative Assembly shall be entitled in the prescribed manner to nominate any eligible person.

"Every person duly qualified to vote for the election of a member of the Legislative Assembly shall be qualified and entitled to vote for the election of Representatives of Victoria.

"The voting shall be taken throughout Victoria as one electoral district, and every voter shall vote for the full number of Representatives required, otherwise the vote shall be rejected as informal.

"No person shall vote or attempt to vote more than once at the same election of Representatives of Victoria."

(A similar provision applies to the subsequent referendum.)

"When the Constitution has been framed by the Convention, copies thereof shall be supplied to the Members of the Convention, and the President shall declare the sitting of the Convention adjourned to a time and place to be fixed by the Convention, not being less than sixty nor more than one hundred and twenty days thereafter. And as soon as convenient the draft constitution shall be submitted for consideration to each House of Parliament sitting in Committee of the whole, and such amendments as may be desired by the Legislature, together with the draft Constitution, shall be remitted to the Convention through the Senior Representative.

"On the reassembling of the Convention the Constitution as framed prior to the adjournment shall be reconsidered, together with such suggested amendments as shall have been forwarded by the various Legislatures, and the Constitution so framed shall be finally adopted with any amendments that may be agreed to."

"So soon as practicable after the close of the proceedings of the Convention the question of the acceptance or rejection of the Constitution shall be referred and submitted to the vote of all persons in Victoria qualified and entitled to vote for the election of Members of the Legislative Assembly."

"The majority of votes shall decide the question, and if the Constitution be thereby rejected, no further action shall be taken pursuant to this Act : Provided that any number of votes in the affirmative less than fifty thousand shall be equivalent to the rejection of the Bill.

"If two Colonies in addition to Victoria accept the Constitution the Legislative Council and the Legislative Assembly of Victoria may adopt a Joint Address to the Queen praying that the Constitution may be passed into law by the Imperial Parliament upon receipt from the Parliaments of such two Colonies, either of similar joint or separate Addresses from each House of such Parliaments."

It will be noticed that the Convention will have entire freedom in regard to any amendments suggested by the Provincial Parliaments, and that if the Constitution be accepted, the Victorian Parliament will not be bound to join in submitting it for Imperial enactment. It is assumed that it will bow to the popular pronouncement unless the Government should have some grave reason for recommending a contrary course. A difficulty, not provided against in the Act, might arise if the Constitution were to be amended during its passage through the Imperial Parliament.

The Act passed by Western Australia provided for the election of the delegates by the two Houses of Parliament sitting as one Chamber, the area of selection being limited to candidates nominated by not less than twenty persons who are qualified to vote at elections for Members of the Assembly. "The draft Constitution, as finally adopted by the Convention, if approved by Parliament, shall be submitted for the decision of the electors of Western Australia by their vote; and if a majority of the electors voting on such question signify their approval of such Constitution, the same may be adopted by the Colony, provided that any number of votes in the affirmative less than six thousand shall be equivalent to the rejection of the Constitution." "The adoption of the Constitution by Western Australia may be signified by the passing of an Act or by a joint resolution of both Houses of

Parliament, and both Houses may thereupon adopt Addresses to the Queen, praying that the Constitution may be passed into law by the Imperial Parliament, subject to the adoption of similar Addresses by at least two other Colonies, of which New South Wales shall be one." Parliament thus retains the initiative in each successive phase of the movement, but will have no power to alter the Bill when it finally leaves the Convention. If the provisions are regarded as unacceptable, it will be able to decline to submit the Bill to the electorate.

The Western Australian measure was based in its general language upon that previously introduced in Queensland, but differed from it in several important particulars. In the latter case it was proposed that the election of the delegates should be vested in the members of the Assembly alone, that, of the ten delegates, five should be chosen by the Southern, three by the Northern, and two by the Central Parliamentary Representatives, a provision inserted in view of the somewhat divergent interests of different portions of the Province, and that the draft Constitution should be submitted for the consideration of the electors in such manner as Parliament might prescribe. The Bill was passed by the Assembly, in spite of a widespread feeling that Queensland should have followed the course of the other Provinces, and was amended by the Council, which regarded itself as unjustifiably ignored, and provided that it should have an equal share with the Assembly in the appointment of the delegates to the Convention. It is unnecessary to consider the arguments by which the Premier supported his proposal of indirect election, or those put forward by the two Houses during the deadlock which followed upon their disagreement. Finally, when each House had insisted several times upon its attitude, the Bill was laid aside by the Council.

As a result of this action the new movement was blocked at its first step, which was regarded with little anxiety even by those who appreciated the difficulties which were likely to attend the later stages. Great disappointment was felt in Australia, and efforts were made, though in vain, to induce Sir Hugh Nelson to reintroduce the Bill in some form that would be acceptable to both Houses. At the same time public opinion demanded that the Convention should be held, even though one of the Provinces would be unrepresented.

The benefits which would follow Federation are so obvious as scarcely to require enumeration. The Federal Government would be able to deal adequately with the problem of National Defence and to speak authoritatively, to the manifest satisfaction of the Imperial Authorities, upon such matters as the contribution of Australia towards the expenses of the Imperial squadron maintained upon its coast ; the consolidation of the debts would, it has been estimated, enable a million pounds to be saved upon the annual bill of interest ; Inter-

provincial Free Trade would promote intercourse
between neighbours who have hitherto been
estranged by arbitrary lines of demarcation; and
in the words of the Chief Justice of Queensland,[1]
"The first effect in point of importance, though
some time may elapse before the effect is fully felt,
will be the creation of an Australian Nation, forming a distinct constituent part of the British Empire,
having one mind, speaking with one voice instead
of the six, often discordant and sometimes inarticu-
late, voices now heard, consulted on all matters of
Imperial concern, and exercising a powerful influence in the political affairs of the whole world."
Such would appear to be the destiny of Australia,
which has, however, doubtless been benefited by
the independent development of its component
parts. In the absence of distinctions of race and
language, in the general diffusion of the Roman
Catholics among the Protestants, and the steady
determination to exclude coloured races, the early
establishment of Federal relations would have produced among Australians a monotonous uniformity
of characteristics, which has to some extent been
prevented by the divergent political tendencies of
the several Provinces.

But, to put the practical question, what are the
prospects of Federation? The general impression
is not one of hopefulness: it is pointed out that the

[1] "Notes on Australian Federation," by Sir S. W. Griffith.
Parliamentary Paper, Queensland, 1896.

Provinces have so long maintained an independent existence that they are unlikely to submit to a curtailment of their powers except under the imperative impulse of the fear of foreign invasion ; that all but the leading politicians realise that they would be affected prejudicially by a change which would dwarf the Legislatures with which they are connected ; that many, especially during the period of depression, dread the creation of a new taxing and governing body ; and that the Labour members, in the natural belief that their influence would be smaller in a Federal Parliament, are either apathetic or actively hostile. The economic aspects of Intercolonial Free Trade, in reference to its probable effect upon the prosperity of manufacturers and producers in the different Provinces, also form an important factor in the situation. Time alone can show whether popular participation in the successive stages of the movement, though it will not be universal, will generate an enthusiasm sufficient to outweigh the opposing forces and weld Australia into a strong and united Nation.

APPENDIX TO IX.

THE NEW FEDERAL SCHEME.[1]

Now that the Adelaide Convention has completed its labours, it is possible to give a connected view of the provisions of the draft Constitution Bill, as it will be submitted to the local

[1] An article published in the Melbourne *Argus* of April 26, 1897, and included with the kind permission of the London agents of that newspaper.

Parliament, and then after it has been again dealt with by a second meeting of the Convention at Sydney, to the vote of the people.

The Bill provides for the constitution of the Commonwealth of Australia and for the appointment of a governor-general by the Queen, at a salary of £10,000. The Federal Parliament is to consist of two Houses—the Senate and the House of Representatives. The former chamber will be composed of six members for each state. They are to be elected by the electors of the Legislative Assembly in each colony for a term of six years, and one-half will retire every three years. For the election of these senators each colony will be regarded as one electorate, and no one will be allowed to vote at more than one polling-booth on the day of election. In other words, the election will be conducted on the same lines as the recent election of representatives to the Federation Convention. At the first meeting of the Senate, the members elected for each state will be divided by lot into two classes, and the seats of those in the first class are to be vacated at the end of the third year, but the others will continue to be members of that House for the full term of six years. In this way one-half the members of the Senate will be elected by the people every third year.

The House of Representatives is to be composed of members directly chosen by the people of the several states, and the number which each colony will return will depend on its population. This Chamber is, as nearly as practicable, to contain double the number of members of the Senate. The House of Representatives would therefore consist, at the outset, of about seventy-two members, which would give as nearly as possible, one member for every 50,000 of the population. Victoria would, roughly speaking, have about twenty-two members. In order, however, to protect the interests of the smaller states in this House, it is provided that Tasmania, South Australia, and Western Australia, shall be entitled to at least five members each, although on the population basis, the island colony might not be able to claim more than four members. Until the Federal Parliament otherwise provides, each local or state Parliament can determine into how many electoral divisions the colony should be divided for the purpose of returning members to the House of Representatives, but should it not divide the state into electoral districts, then each colony is to be regarded as one electorate, in the same way as in the case of the election of senators.

The duration of every House of Representatives will be three years, unless it is sooner dissolved by the Governor-General. There is no power, however, conferred on the Governor-General to dissolve the Senate. The qualification of electors of members of the House of Representatives is in each state to be that for electors of the more numerous House—or Legislative Assembly—of the state. The members of both Houses are to receive an allowance of £400 each per annum for their services.

The following are the subjects the Commonwealth Parliament is to be empowered to legislate upon and deal with :—

1. The regulation of trade and commerce with other countries and among the several states.
2. Customs and excise and bounties.
3. Raising money by any other mode or system of taxation.
4. Borrowing money on the public credit of the commonwealth.
5. Postal and telegraphic services.
6. The military and naval defence of the commonwealth and the several states, and the calling out of the forces to execute and maintain the laws of the commonwealth.
7. Munitions of war.
8. Navigation and shipping.
9. Ocean beacons and buoys and ocean lighthouses and lightships.
10. Astronomical and meteorological observations.
11. Quarantine.
12. Fisheries in Australian waters beyond territorial limits.
13. Census and statistics.
14. Currency, coinage, and legal tender.
15. Banking, the incorporation of banks, and the issue of paper money.
16. Insurance, excluding state insurance not extending beyond the limits of the state concerned.
17. Weights and measures.
18. Bills of exchange and promissory notes.
19. Bankruptcy and insolvency.
20. Copyrights and patents of inventions, designs, and trade marks.

21. Naturalisation and aliens.
22. Foreign corporations, and trading or financial corporations, formed in any state or part of the commonwealth.
23. Marriage and divorce.
24. Parental rights, and the custody and guardianship of infants.
25. The service and execution throughout the commonwealth of the civil and criminal process and judgments of the courts of the states.
26. The recognition throughout the commonwealth of the laws, the public acts and records, and the judicial proceedings of the states.
27. Immigration and emigration.
28. The influx of criminals.
29. External affairs and treaties.
30. The relations of the commonwealth to the islands of the Pacific.
31. The control and regulation of the navigation of the River Murray, and the use of the waters thereof from where it first forms the boundary between Victoria and New South Wales to the sea.
32. The control of railways with respect to transport for the military purposes of the commonwealth.
33. The taking over by the commonwealth, with the consent of the state, of the whole or any part of the railways of any state or states, upon such terms as may be arranged between the commonwealth and the state.
34. Railway construction and extension with the consent of any state or states concerned.
35. Matters referred to the Parliament of the commonwealth by the Parliament or Parliaments of any state or states, but so that the law shall extend only to the state or states by whose Parliament or Parliaments the matter was referred, and to such other states as may afterwards adopt the law.
36. The exercise within the commonwealth, at the request or with the concurrence of the Parliaments of all the states concerned, of any legislative powers which can at the establishment of this constitution be exercised only by the Parliament of the United Kingdom, or by the Federal Council of Australasia.
37. Any matters necessary for, or incidental to, the carrying

into execution of the foregoing powers or of any other powers vested by this constitution in the Parliament or the Executive Government of the commonwealth, or in any department or officer thereof.

All matters not mentioned above, such as land settlement, railway construction, &c., are to remain vested in the Parliaments of the several states. Each state shall retain its local Parliament and have a Governor, who is to be appointed by the Crown, and communicate direct with the Crown as at present.

On the establishment of the commonwealth the control of the following departments will be taken over by the Federal Government, and the commonwealth will assume the obligations of any state or states with respect to such matters :—

Customs and excise.

Posts and telegraphs.

Military and naval defence.

Ocean beacons, buoys, lighthouses.

Quarantine.

There are to be seven Ministers of State, and their salaries will, in the aggregate, be £12,000 per annum. A Minister, within three months after being appointed to that office, must become a member of one of the Houses of the Federal Parliament.

All Bills having for their main object the appropriation of any part of the public revenue, or moneys, or the imposition of any tax, must originate in the House of Representatives. Bills imposing taxation must deal with the imposition of taxation only, and those imposing duties of Customs or excise must deal with duties of Customs or excise only. The expenditure for services other than the ordinary annual services of the Government must not be authorised by the same law as that which appropriates the supplies for the ordinary annual services, but must be authorised by a separate measure. The Senate can amend any Bills except those imposing taxation, or appropriating the necessary supplies for the ordinary annual services of the Government. With respect to these money measures, the Senate can, at any stage, return a taxation or appropriation Bill to the House of Representatives, suggesting that any provision or item therein should be omitted or amended, and the House of Representatives may, if it thinks fit, make such omissions or amendments with or without modifications. The Bill, in its amended or original form—should the House of Representatives decline to adopt the suggestion of the Senate—will then be sent back to the latter Chamber, which may either pass or reject the measure.

The seat of the Government of the commonwealth is to be determined by the Federal Parliament. Until such determination the Parliament shall be summoned to meet at such place as the majority of the Governors of the states, or, in the event of an equal division of opinion amongst them, as the Governor-General may direct.

Before the Constitution can be amended an absolute majority of both the House of Representatives and Senate must approve of the alteration, and it must then be confirmed by a vote of the people, a majority of the states being required as well as a majority of the people.

There is to be a federal judiciary, consisting of a high court of Australia, and such inferior courts as Parliament may determine. The high court is to consist of a chief justice, and at least four other judges, and is to hear appeals from the state courts and inferior federal courts. This appeal is to be final, except that in matters affecting the public interests of the commonwealth or of any state, application may be made to the Queen for special leave to appeal to the Privy Council.

Uniform Customs duties are to be imposed within two years of the establishment of the commonwealth, and trade and intercourse throughout the commonwealth is then to be absolutely free. In the meantime the local tariffs are to continue, but they will be collected by the Federal Government, and after deducting from the revenue received in each state the contribution of that state towards federal expenses, the balance is to be returned to the state month by month. During the first three years after federation the total annual expenditure of the Federal Government is to be limited to £300,000 for new federal expenses, and £1,250,000 for services transferred from the states. During the first five years after the imposition of a uniform tariff, the surplus revenue, after deducting the contribution of each state to the federal expenses, is to be returned to the states in the following way : Accounts of Customs and excise duties collected in each state are to be kept during the twelve months following the coming into operation of the uniform tariff, in order to ascertain, first the average net amount per head in each state, and next the average per head for the whole commonwealth. A sliding scale, extending over four years, is then to be adopted, in order to determine the amount to be returned. Where the average for a particular state for the first year is less than the general average, the per capita sum is to be increased by equal gradations, until, at the end of four years, it equals the general average. Similarly, where the average for a state is greater than the general average, it is to be gradually reduced to the general average. Then, at the end of the five-year period, all the states will be placed on the same footing, and will receive an equal sum per head from the federal revenue. This scheme of distribution is subject, however, to the important proviso that during the five years the aggregate amount returned to all the states in any year must not be less than the aggregate amount returned in the year immediately preceding the imposition of uniform duties.

Equality of trade is to be preserved throughout the commonwealth, and any law or regulation derogating from that principle is to be null and void. Parliament may appoint an inter-state commission to execute and maintain upon railways within the commonwealth, and upon rivers flowing through, in, or between two or more states the provisions of the constitution relating to trade and commerce. The commission is to have such powers of adjudication and administration as may be necessary for its purposes, and as the Parliament may from time to time determine, but shall have no powers in reference to the rates or regulations of any railway in any state, except in cases of rates or regulations preferential in effect, and made and used for the purpose of drawing traffic to that railway from the railway of a neighbouring state.

X

SALIENT FEATURES OF THE AUSTRALASIAN DEMOCRACY

Indirect effects of the discovery of gold—Causes of the financial crisis—The origin and extent of State Socialism—The thriftiness of the working-classes—Labour Representation in Parliament—Parliamentary Government—Direct Taxation—Conciliation and Arbitration in Industrial disputes—Protection and its corollaries — The feeling towards Great Britain — General conclusions.

T HE enormous immigration of the fifties, due to the great discoveries of gold in Victoria and New South Wales, has caused Australia to become one of the most democratic countries in the world. Before that time the soil was held in large areas by pastoralists who, in the absence of opposing forces, would have formed themselves gradually into a strong landed aristocracy. But the miners, a class of men who had shown their energy and determination by their readiness to travel thousands of miles in the search for wealth, introduced an entirely new element : they had thrown off their traditionary reverence for vested institutions, they were able to earn high wages or directly to enrich themselves,

and they resented an assumption of superiority on
the part of any section in the community. When,
in the course of years, the mining industry began to
wane, they swarmed into the towns and constituted
an important link in the chain of causes which has
swelled some of the capitals to their present un-
wieldy dimensions. Deprived of their means of
livelihood, and indisposed for rural life, they
clamoured for other employment, and were able,
in several Provinces, to induce the Ministry to
impose a protective tariff which artificially fostered
the growth of manufactures. The protective tariff
naturally increased the urban population, as did the
undiscriminative system of State-aided immigration,
the centralisation of all departments of the Government, and, in its ultimate effects, the construction
of public works.

In a population of pastoralists and miners,
engaged in pursuits which inculcate reliance upon
individual efforts, it is somewhat strange to note the
early development of a tendency towards State
socialism ; but I am inclined to think that, in this
respect also, the discoveries of gold exercised a permanent influence, not only in the Provinces immediately affected, but throughout Australasia, from a
tendency towards imitation. In the first years of
Responsible Government British capitalists had a
natural distrust of Australian securities, and declined
to advance money except at a high rate of interest.
But when they saw the phenomenal increase in the

yield of gold, and the large revenue obtained from the sale of lands, they overcame their scruples and displayed, during the twenty years which preceded the financial crisis, a readiness to grant loans to the several Governments which is believed by many to have been a great misfortune to their debtors.

The political and unremunerative railways of Victoria, which have been discussed in the chapter dealing with that Province, could not have been constructed but for the easy access to large funds. Another aspect of the question has been emphasised in an article published by the Sydney *Bulletin* [1] which, however much an Englishman may demur to its Republican principles, must be admitted to be an authority on Australasian topics. A strong plea is put forward for the necessity of defining by Act of Parliament what kind of works should be charged to loan-moneys, and what should be charged to revenue. The advantages, it is contended, will be threefold; the attention of the country will be drawn to the matter; the Loan Estimates go through so rapidly that very few people are aware how the thing is worked. The lender will know the destination of his money, and all treasurers will be placed on a level, whereas, at present, "the dishonest treasurer who makes a surplus by using borrowed money for road repairs and all manner of other ordinary expenditure is a heaven-born financier, while the honest one who doesn't is driven out of

[1] August 8, 1896.

office, either for having a deficit, or for increasing taxation, and is a failure either way." Official figures are quoted for New South Wales in order to prove that during the years 1885-1890, which covered the flotation of several loans, surpluses and deficits alternated as the treasurer was or was not able to dispose of borrowed funds. Indirectly, of course, many of the public works which do not produce a direct revenue may be of financial benefit to the State, through an increase of population and the encouragement of settlement; but it is a hazardous principle to borrow money for their construction.

Equally dangerous for Australia was the more recent excessive eagerness of the British capitalist to invest his money in Australian commercial undertakings, as, according to the Victorian Year Book,[1] a publication of the highest merit, "there is no doubt that the feverish financial activity that preceded, and ultimately led to, the Australian financial crisis primarily arose from the enormous influx of British capital—far in excess of the legitimate requirements of the Colonies—for remunerative enterprises. This influx was probably the result of the large amount of attention that for some years prior to 1888 had been directed to these Colonies, which were brought into prominence by such events as the passing of the first Federal Council Act by the Imperial Parliament in 1885, the Colonial and Indian Exhibition held in London in 1886, and the Imperial

[1] 1893, vol. ii. pp. 456, 457.

Conference in 1887; it was also much stimulated by
the lowering in 1888 of the interest on the British
Public Debt, and *pro rata* on other first-class British
securities. The first indications of this were noticeable in the marked rise in the prices of all Colonial
Government securities which occurred just after Mr.
Goschen's notification of his scheme for reducing
the interest on the National Debt of the United
Kingdom, in March, 1888. Such securities, however, being of limited extent, the superabundant
capital was forced into private channels, which led
to the growth of co-operative enterprise on an un-
precedented scale—through the medium of joint
stock companies—which commenced prior to, but
probably in anticipation of, the conversion of the
British Public Debt, and culminated in the United
Kingdom, as well as in Australia, in the same year.
Owing to this increasing competition for Colonial
Government securities, and the consequent fall in
the rate of interest thereon, the Colonial Governments were tempted to, and no doubt did, borrow
in excess of their immediate requirements, although
this was not recognised during the period of general
inflation; but assuming a portion of the Government loans to have been unjustified, far worse was the
condition of the large private investments, chiefly in
joint stock companies, many of which supplemented
their resources by deposits—equivalent in some
cases to as much as three times the paid-up capital
—which had been drawn, by reason of the high rates

of interest offered, from all sections of the community, both in England and Australia. Between the 1st of January, 1887, and the 30th of June, 1893, but for the most part in 1888, 1,154 companies with a paid-up capital of no less than £28,436,500 (subscribed capital £54,300,000) were registered in Victoria alone, and of these, 397, with a paid-up capital of £9,469,000 (subscribed capital £19,526,000) are known to have become defunct, to say nothing of numerous others, of which no information has been furnished to the Registrar-General." The crisis was most acute in Victoria, but its effects were felt largely, and are still felt in calls upon shareholders, in other Provinces. In conclusion, while British capitalists are still chary of industrial investments, they appear to be willing to meet the Australasian Governments in their resumption of applications for loans.

The danger is accentuated by the tendency towards State socialism, the origin of which I had begun to discuss before this long digression. The earliest concessions for the construction of railways were granted in New South Wales in 1848 and 1853, but the companies were unable to carry out their undertakings, owing to the scarcity of workmen caused by the rush to the goldfields, and the Government stepped in and completed the railways out of public funds. This assumption by the State of a function which had been delegated to private enterprise, coupled with the growing confidence of the British investor and the elasticity of the revenue, both from the Customs and from the disposal of land, which had been accelerated by the rapid increase of population, appears to have convinced the political leaders of the advisability of the Governmental extension of the railway lines. They were enabled to carry out this policy without difficulty, as the bulk of the electors were engrossed in material pursuits and did not trouble themselves about political issues. In Victoria three short lines of railways were constructed during the fifties by private companies, but were subsequently purchased by the Government, which thenceforward monopolised the construction of new lines. Why Victoria and the other Provinces should have decided in favour of State ownership and management of railways I am unable to explain, except upon the hypothesis that they were influenced by the example of New South Wales, that they wished to open up the country more quickly than would otherwise have been possible, and that they were tempted by the funds at their disposal in surpluses of revenue over expenditure. Then, the railways having in many instances preceded population, it was necessary, if the lines were not to be unprofitable, that special steps should be taken in order to promote settlement. This was done, partly by the offer of land upon favourable conditions, partly by the payment out of the National Exchequer of all the expenses of Local Government. In New South Wales this state of things still prevails in many of the rural districts; in

the other Provinces *pro rata* subsidies are paid to the
Local Authorities, but are limited, in some cases, to
a fixed term of years. The Local Bodies have had
no spontaneous evolution ; they are the creation of
the Central Government, they are supported and
controlled by it, and look to it for assistance whenever they are in financial difficulties. It would seem
that, accustomed to State railways and to depen-
dency upon the State in their local affairs, Austra-
lasians have been led insensibly to magnify the
efficacy of its intervention and to welcome every
enlargement of its sphere of action. The protective
tariff appears to have had a similar effect, unless it
is to be regarded as a mere coincidence that South
Australia, New Zealand, and Victoria, which alone
are avowedly Protectionist, have authorised the
widest extension of the functions of the State.

Throughout Australasia all parties in the several
Parliaments are agreed on the principle of the State
ownership of railways. In Victoria and Queensland the railways are entirely in the hands of the
Government ; in New South Wales and South
Australia they are so with some trifling exceptions ;
in Tasmania, Western Australia, and New Zealand
a few private lines have been authorised because it
has been advisable, in the interests of settlement,
that they should be constructed, and the Governments have been unable or unwilling to undertake
further financial obligations. The recent action of
Western Australia may be mentioned in evidence of

the prevalent feeling, it having taken advantage of
its improved credit to purchase one of the private
lines. The waterworks of the capitals, also, are
national or municipal property; but other municipal
monopolies, such as gasworks and tramways, are
mostly in the hands of private companies.

The railways of Australasia are worked, as far as
is consonant with national interests, for the direct
benefit of producers, who, as has been seen in the
chapters dealing with individual Provinces, have
been the special object of the paternal solicitude
of their Governments. The various efforts in this
direction may briefly be recapitulated. South Australia, Victoria, Western Australia, and New Zealand
make advances to settlers at low rates of interest;
South Australia sells its wines in London; Queensland facilitates the erection of sugar mills, and is
proposing to establish depôts in London and the
provinces for the receipt and distribution of its
frozen meat; Victoria and South Australia have
given a bonus upon the exportation of dairy produce. These Provinces and New Zealand receive
such produce, grade and freeze it free of charge or
at a rate which barely covers the expenses. Victoria
has given subsidies towards the erection of butter
factories; Victoria and New Zealand have subsidised
the mining industry; and Western Australia has
adopted a comprehensive scheme for the supply of
water to the Coolgardie Goldfields.

The above brief summary shows that action by

the State for the promotion of enterprise has met
with approval in Queensland and Western Australia
as well as in the Provinces which have adopted the
widest extensions of the franchise. It may be noted,
however, that Sir Hugh Nelson, the Premier of
Queensland, is an individualist at heart, and consents
to extensions of the functions of the State un-
willingly upon a conviction of their necessity;
while, in Western Australia, Sir John Forrest is a
strong advocate of State socialism, and opposed to
private enterprise in any matter which is of the
nature of a monopoly. New South Wales and
Tasmania have not hitherto followed the lead of
the other Provinces. This tendency is one of the
most marked of recent years, and received a strong
impetus from the financial crisis of 1893, which
burst the bubble of a fictitious prosperity and compelled attention to the strenuous development of
the resources of the soil. It is likely to lead to
closer relations between the Provinces, from the
appreciation of the fact that the exports of one
Province, if unregulated and allowed to fall into
disrepute, may prejudicially affect the interests of
the whole continent.

As regards the invervention of the State in the
direction of industrial legislation, the Governments
of Western Australia and Tasmania have had little
cause to take action, in the absence of crowded
centres and of manufacturing activity; but New
South Wales, Victoria, Queensland, South Australia,

and New Zealand have placed stringent Factory Acts upon their Statute Books. Measures have also been passed, largely under the influence of Labour Representatives, dealing with the liability of employers, the regulation of mines, the protection of shop assistants, and other matters affecting the welfare of the working classes. Upon their enactment complaints have been made of undue interference with employers ; but the administration is now, in most cases, carried out efficiently and without unnecessary friction.

Indirectly, the various Provinces have, through their schemes of public works, exercised considerable influence upon the demand for labour and have, upon the completion of the more important undertakings, been subject to continual pressure with the object of inducing them to authorise special works for the benefit of those who have been deprived of their livelihood. New South Wales, indeed, and, to a lesser extent, Victoria, have almost admitted an obligation to provide work or rations for the unemployed. In Victoria the tension has been relaxed by the formation of the Labour Colony of Leongatha, at which the destitute can obtain temporary subsistence. Australian politicians, generally, were appalled by the undeserved misery which resulted from the cessation of public works and from the financial disturbances, and, under the stress of humanitarian motives, failed to temper their humanity with discretion, and initiated a policy of indiscriminate assistance from which, once entered upon, it has been difficult for them to draw back. The formation of village settlements in all the Provinces except Western Australia was based upon the necessity for special efforts in the face of the prevailing distress. Australians have never been able to regard the unemployed as a necessary factor in their economic system. The ordinary problems of pauperism have been felt acutely in Australasia and have been met in somewhat similar fashion in the different Provinces. Destitute children are, in most cases, boarded out; the aged and incapable are provided for in Benevolent Asylums. In Victoria, New South Wales, and New Zealand a movement has recently arisen for the adoption of a system of old-age pensions, which has had no appreciable results in the former Province, but has led in New South Wales to the appointment of a Parliamentary Committee which reported favourably and suggested forms of additional taxation by which the necessary funds might be obtained, and in New Zealand to the introduction of a Ministerial measure which sought to establish the general principle and left to the House the elaboration of the financial details. The Bill was accepted on its second reading, but in Committee an amendment was carried against the Government to the effect that all persons above the age of sixty-five, irrespectively of their means, should be entitled to receive a pension. An Act was, however, subsequently passed of which the

object is to ascertain the probable cost of a pension
fund. All persons of the age of sixty-five and
upwards, who have resided in the Province for
twenty years, imprisonment being reckoned as
absence, and are not possessed of an income exceeding £50 a year, are entitled to apply for a
pension certificate which will be issued to them
upon the verification of their claims, and will be
regarded as conclusive if a pension fund be established hereafter. The success of the Government
at the recent elections renders it probable that the
matter will shortly receive attention. In neither of
the Provinces in which the subject has been discussed is it proposed that the pension should be
earned by previous contributions; it is to be
offered as a free gift in recognition of the services
which every worker must have rendered to the
community.

To conclude a superficial summary of the functions undertaken, or likely to be undertaken, by
the State in Australasia, it may be mentioned that
the State system of primary education is in all the
Provinces compulsory and undenominational. In
South Australia, Victoria, Queensland, and New
Zealand it is also free; in the other Provinces
fees are charged but may be remitted, wholly or
partly, in the case of the inability of parents to
pay them. There are no signs that the advocates
of grants in aid of denominational education are
gaining ground; in the direct reference to the

electors taken in South Australia they were defeated by a large majority, and have equally little chance of securing subsidies to religious bodies.

In the presence of great activity on the part of the State, it is interesting to note to what extent the working classes have exerted themselves on their own behalf. Distributive co-operation has not become popular owing, partly, according to the *Australasian*,[1] "to the vicissitudes in trade which are inseparable from new countries, and to the temptations which are consequently held out to the workers from time to time to change their occupations and abodes. Partly, too, an explanation may be found in the efficacy of existing agencies for distribution. But we cannot help thinking that it is due also, in part, to the pernicious ideas which lead so many of our artisans to cry out against capital, and to seek the aid of the State, instead of trusting to their own efforts and determining to become capitalists themselves in a way which has been proved by the co-operative societies at home to be thoroughly practical." Though the *Australasian* is strongly individualistic in its bias, it appears to be justified in its reference to a certain lack of initiative shown by Australasian workmen; they are inclined to look upon the State as a gold mine from which they can draw permanent dividends, especially as they are scarcely, if at all, affected directly by the periodical calls upon the

[1] July 25, 1896.

shareholders; but, in his strictures upon the attitude of labour towards capital, the writer should have added that the wealthy classes are at least as ready to misjudge every effort made by the Labour Representatives to pass remedial measures through the legislatures. Proceeding to deal with the co-operation of producers, he says that "there is co-operation of this kind already in our butter and cheese factories, where the farmer who conveys his produce to the factory may also be a shareholder, and at the end of the half-year may receive a dividend on his shares and a bonus on the milk supplied, in addition to the established price. Co-operation of a like kind prevails, to some extent, though not so largely as might be desired, between the graziers and the companies for the export of Australian meat." These remarks, which refer primarily to Victoria, are generally true of Australasia.

But, while the working classes look constantly to the State for assistance in various forms, they can be shown to have made considerable provision against the future. In spite of bad times, the number of depositors in Australasian Savings Banks rose from 742,000 in 1891 to 895,000 in 1895, and the total amount of deposits from 19 to 26 millions. Victoria and South Australia, which are followed closely by New Zealand, have the largest number of depositors in proportion to population, 29 and 24 per 100 respectively, and Queensland and New

South Wales the highest average amount of deposits.[1] In the three Provinces, therefore, in which the paternal action of the Government is carried to the furthest extent, we find the widest diffusion of an important exemplification of the spirit of thrift. I am far from suggesting a relation of cause and effect, as the amount of savings must depend largely upon the rate of wages, the abundance or scarcity of employment, the cost of living, and many other factors, and would merely point out that the policy in question does not appear to have deterred the working classes from individual efforts.

As regards Friendly Societies, South Australia takes the lead with a membership exceeding one in ten of the population; Victoria comes next with one in fifteen, and is third in the average amount of funds per member. Under the latter head New Zealand occupied the first place with £18 8s. 2d., and is followed by Western Australia with £17 10s. 4d., but the latter amount is of no comparative importance owing to the very small number of subscribers.[2]

In 1895 the average amount of assurance per head of the population in Australasia was £20, the average sum assured per policy £285, and the average number of policies per 1,000 of the population, 70. Compared with the United Kingdom,

[1] "A Statistical Account of the Seven Colonies of Australasia, 1895-6," by T. A. Coghlan, p. 345.
[2] Ibid., p. 359.

Australasia has a considerable advantage in the first of these figures, has the proportion reversed in the second, but wins by more than two to one on the last, which is the most interesting as a further indication of the prevalence of the instinct of providence among Australasian workmen.[1]

Prior to the recent crisis the working classes had availed themselves largely of the opportunities which Building Societies offered to them to secure the freehold of their homes by payments spread over a term of years ; but a run upon the deposits lodged in these institutions, which set in towards the end of 1891, and continued during 1892, affected them disastrously, and the large majority of even the soundest of them were obliged eventually, owing to the heavy withdrawal of deposits, to close their doors. Though some have since been re-opened, upon terms agreed to between the shareholders and depositors, their business has collapsed for the time, the amount of advances in Victoria having fallen from over two millions in 1890 and in 1891 to less than a hundred thousand pounds in 1893.[2] In the apparent absence of statistics of the number of freeholders in several Provinces, no general idea can be formed of the extent to which the working classes have, through Building Societies and otherwise, invested their savings in the acquisition of

---

[1] "A Statistical Account of the Seven Colonies of Australasia, 1895–6," p. 357.　　[2] Victorian Year Book, 1894, p. 648.

freehold properties. The only figures that I have
been able to obtain give the estimated number of
owners as 30,600, 91,500, and 184,500 for New
South Wales, New Zealand, and Victoria respectively. As far as the two latter Provinces are
concerned, the total populations being only
699,000 and 1,174,000, it is absurd to suppose
that the electors, a large proportion of whom are
freeholders, will be captivated by the advocates of
the Single Tax. It cannot too often be repeated
that the Australasian Governments, all of which
are, to a greater or lesser degree, aiming at the
multiplication of small owners or perpetual leaseholders, are rendering it practically impossible
that an agitation for the confiscation of land values
should be successful, and are fostering the growth
of that class of settlers which is believed to be
Conservative in the best sense of the word. But
large estates, except in the case of certain kinds
of pastoral land, are doomed to extinction, either
in the natural course of events, owing to the
costliness of labour, or from the pressure of heavy
graduated taxation, the workmen of Australasia
being thoroughly convinced of its justice as a
means of raising revenue and of its efficacy as
a means of causing land to be subdivided or
placed upon the market. They have also, as has
been seen, supported legislation which has authorised the re-purchase and subdivision of landed
estates.

Lastly, they have realised since 1890 that, for the furtherance of their aspirations, the strength of their Unions should be devoted mainly to the promotion of the representation of Labour in Parliament. The great strike of that year has been described so fully that it is unnecessary to say more than that a strong combination of labour, which had made itself master of the situation, was confronted upon the outbreak of hostilities by rapidly organised but powerful associations of employers; that the struggle, which spread over the whole Continent and New Zealand, terminated in the success of the latter, and that the workmen realised that, even had they succeeded, the victory would have been won at too heavy a cost in the misery entailed upon themselves and their families. Many of them were dissatisfied with the generalship of their leaders during the strike, and realised that the exhaustion of their funds rendered them unable to engage again in a huge industrial struggle. In the following years low prices, the financial crisis, and the consequent scarcity of employment and fall in wages, further weakened the Unions and intensified the conviction that strikes should be superseded by the ballot-box. In some Provinces, also, it was felt that the rivalry of parties had degenerated into a contest between the ins and the outs, and that progressive measures would not be passed until Labour had entered as a compact body into the arena.

I have discussed in the earlier chapters the

history and results of Labour representation in several of the Provinces, and have shown that the Labour Party has been successful in South Australia, where it has formed an alliance with the Government, though maintaining a separate organisation, and in New South Wales, where it has held the balance of power between the Protectionists and Free Traders, but has failed utterly in Queensland, where mainly through its own fault, but partly through the astuteness of its opponents, it has occupied a position of antagonism to all the vested interests of the community. In Victoria the Labour Party acts usually with the Government, but seeks to obtain its objects by the exercise of its strength more than by friendly negotiations. In New Zealand no distinct Party was formed, but the working-men representatives threw in their lot with the Government and, by consistent support, helped to secure the imposition of graduated taxation and the enactment, among other measures, of a compulsory Conciliation and Arbitration Act, and of a large number of Industrial Statutes.

A great similarity of aims and aspirations can be traced between the different Labour Parties if we ignore side issues and exclude that of Queensland, which is affected by the taint of aggressive socialism. Judging from the respective programmes and from conversations which I have had with many of the leaders, I find that, subject to certain exceptions which I shall mention, they are united upon the following propositions :—

Manhood or adult suffrage, shorn of the plural vote, should be the basis of representation in the Assembly. The Legislative Council should be abolished, as it prevents the wishes of the people from being carried into effect.

Direct taxation should consist of graduated death duties and graduated taxes on incomes and land values.

Parliament should secure to every worker for wages sanitary and safe conditions of employment, and immunity from excessive hours of labour.

Machinery should be provided by Parliament by which industrial disputes may be referred to an impartial tribunal.

The workers should protect themselves not only against foreign goods, but against undesirable immigrants, whether they be Orientals or indigent Europeans.

The consideration of these questions, and of the wider issues with which they are concerned, will cover most of the points of recent interest in Australasian politics.

(1) It is doubtful whether Responsible Government, in the sense of government by a Ministry which carries out a definite policy approved by the country, and, in return, receives allegiance from its

supporters in Parliament, has ever been acclimatised
in Australasia except in New South Wales under the
influence of the late Sir Henry Parkes. How, indeed, could it be otherwise, when it was sought to
transplant a delicate system, hallowed by conventions
and dependent for its success upon the election of a
special class of representatives, among a community
necessarily ruled by men who had little experience
of public life ? Australian Parliaments, save on the
rare occasions when some important issue, such
as that of the tariff, has come to the front, have not
been divided on ordinary party lines, and have
amused themselves with the excitement of a constant succession of new Ministries selected on
personal and not on political considerations. New
South Wales, South Australia, and Victoria, to take
three Provinces at random, have had, respectively,
28, 42, and 26 Ministries in 40 years. The policy of
the Opposition has often been almost identical with
that of the Government. Again, coalitions between
former opponents have been of frequent occurrence;
the Ministries formed by Messrs. Deakin and Gillies
in Victoria, and by Sir Samuel Griffith and Sir
Thomas McIlwraith in Queensland, are recent
instances of this tendency. In some rural constituencies, also, candidates appeal to the electorate
on personal grounds and are not required to declare
their adhesion to a party. I was struck, when present at the elections in South Australia and New
Zealand, by the subsequent animated discussions in

the newspapers as to the probable effect of the changes in the personnel of the Members upon the prospects of the Government. This is the more noticeable from the fact that the freedom of action allowed to representatives has been curtailed since the return to Parliament of Labour Members, who are pledged to a definite programme and have put forward questions on which there is a distinct line of cleavage. Proposals for the extension of the franchise, for the abolition of the plural vote, or for the imposition of a tax on incomes and land values, are such as divide the electorate into two camps and perpetuate the division in the House. This state of things, combined, perhaps, with the financial crisis which raised problems demanding continuity of administration for their solution, has contributed to the greater stability of Ministries. Another factor, which has given constituencies a greater hold on their representatives, and has tended thereby to make them adhere more closely to one or other of the parties, is the payment of Members, which has now been adopted in all the Lower Houses except that of Western Australia, and in the Upper Houses of South Australia, Tasmania, and New Zealand. Australia has been confronted with the difficulty experienced by every young country, that the men who should naturally enter Parliament are prevented by commercial or professional duties from devoting the necessary time, and that, in the absence of men of leisure, constituencies are much hampered in their choice of candidates. The payment of Members, it is needless to say, offers no inducement to the successful merchant or lawyer, but has increased the competition among men to whom the salary is an inducement. My inquiries as to its effect upon the tone of politicians have elicited mutually contradictory replies. On the one hand I am assured that the attractions of the salary have led men to resort to disreputable practices in order to be selected as candidates and to seek to retain the fickle affections of their constituents by similar means; on the other, that necessitous Members have been raised by the salary above temptations which their poverty made it difficult for them to resist ; and such temptations must increase in number with each extension of the functions of the State unless it be dissociated from political influence. It is clear that a knowledge of the inner life of a Parliament could alone supply materials for the adequate discussion of this question, and that a similar consideration applies to the discussion of the effects of State socialism upon political morality. The possible abuses are many : railways may be constructed with a view to popularity ; the rents of Crown tenants may be remitted, and borrowers may be allowed to fall in arrears with the interest on their advances ; subsidies and bonuses voted by Parliament may be misapplied ; and the unemployed may be conciliated by unnecessary public works. Personal corruption, I am confident,

does not exist, but that safeguards have been felt to
be necessary is proved by the appointment of independent Railway Commissioners by New South
Wales, Victoria, South Australia, Queensland, and
New Zealand, and of Public Works Committees by
Victoria and New South Wales.   In the latter country, as has been seen, the Commissioners have been
most successful, but New Zealand has reverted to
the system of political control, and Victoria, Queensland, and South Australia have reduced the number
of Commissioners from three to one.   This change,
which must have lessened the efficacy of non-
political control, was advocated on grounds of
economy at a time when all forms of expenditure
were being cut down to the lowest point.   In
Victoria the Leongatha Labour Settlement has
diminished the difficulties connected with the
unemployed, and its administration has been
studied by the other Provinces with a view to
similar action.   The general political tone is healthy,
and is stimulated, in all the Provinces, by a high-
class press, which uses its great influence in a
conscientious manner.   But, as long as Treasurers
can balance their accounts by recourse to loans, and
are tempted, as is inevitable, to apply borrowed
money to placatory enterprises, the dangers which
are necessarily connected with State socialism are
multiplied tenfold.   They would be lessened if the
objects for which loans might be contracted were
defined, as has been suggested, by Act of Parliament,

or if Federation were to eventuate at an early date and the right to borrow were limited to the Federal Authority.

In New Zealand alone have I found direct evidence of the misuse of political patronage. Upon the third reading of the Appropriation Bill in 1896, Captain Russell, the Leader of the Opposition, made use of the following words : " I maintain that for years past the administration of the Government has been anything but good. They have hunted for popularity and they have hunted their enemies. They have hunted their enemies to a very great extent. You find positions which were capably filled by old and valued servants now filled by friends of the Government. We have a system of espionage in existence which is disgusting. . . The Civil Servants should not depend on the favour and their popularity with Ministers for promotion, but rather on good honest service, and that is not the case now. Why, a Civil Servant dare not come and speak to an Opposition Member for fear of that fact being reported to the Ministers. (An Hon. Member : No !) It is all very well to say 'No,' but I am acquainted with dozens of Civil Servants in Wellington, and they will not come and speak to me in the street for fear of being reported." [1] In his reply the Premier made no attempt to meet these charges, which I have quoted because I have gathered corroborative

[1] Parliamentary Debates of New Zealand, vol. 96, p. 901.

evidence in different parts of the country, though it is not such as admits of being adduced as definite proof, and because the Minister of Lands made an exceedingly candid admission shortly after the elections. In the course of a speech delivered at Geraldine he is reported by a Ministerial newspaper to have said : " They had endeavoured during their term of office to do what they could in the interests of the Colony as a whole, but they had been very badly treated by two classes of the public at the elections. In the session of 1895, they would remember, the Government passed a measure to give relief to pastoral Crown tenants who lost a large number of sheep in the snow. The Government did this in the interest of the people as a whole, as they thought, but how had they been treated by the people they helped in time of distress ? (A voice : Very badly.) Yes, there might have been one or two exceptions, but generally speaking they fought tooth and nail against the Government. Then, again, the Government saved the Bank of New Zealand and the Colony from ruin, but still the old leaven of the Bank fought and voted against the Government at the elections. He considered this very unfair on their part, considering what the Government had done for them." [1] Sir Robert Stout, a former Premier of New Zealand, has also brought a grave indictment against the Government, from

[1] *New Zealand Times*, January 1, 1897.

which I quote the portion referring to appointments :—

" By the Statute Law of New Zealand, no one who has been a member of either House can be appointed to any position in the Civil Service until he has for twelve months ceased to be a member of Parliament. A vacancy occurred in the position of Sergeant-at-arms, and it was announced that an ex-member, who had at the elections retired in favour of a Ministerial candidate, had received the office. When Parliament met, the appointment gave rise to much discussion. Ultimately a large majority supported the Ministry in conferring the appointment temporarily, the official appointment to be made at the end of twelve months. If this had been the only flagrant violation of the law it might have been overlooked ; but it is only a type of what has been done. The Civil Service Reform Act, 1886, provides that no one, save an expert, can be appointed to the Civil Service unless he enters as a cadet. Some departments, such as the railway, postal, and telegraph departments, are exempted from the provisions of the Act. The cadets must obtain their positions by competition ; the examination is annual. The Ministry, however, appointed some cadets out of their order, and some who had never even submitted to an examination at all. There is a provision for " temporary " clerks. When vacancies arise in the service these are given to temporary clerks. The policy of "spoils for the victors" has been openly defended. To carry out this pernicious system the law has been violated. It has been said that only those of the 'right colour' of political opinions should receive appointments in the Civil Service." [1]

However great may be one's sympathy with the efforts of the Government to encourage settlement and to promote industrial conciliation and arbitration, one cannot but rejoice at the increased strength of the Opposition, which will be sufficient to enforce greater purity of administration and the enactment of legislation which will prevent a recurrence of the evil.

The realisation of the dangers of an unmuzzled democracy has caused a widespread anxiety which has been displayed in vehement but, for the most part, unsuccessful opposition to proposed changes in the constitution of the Assembly. New Zealand and South Australia have adopted adult suffrage, coupled with the abolition of plural voting; Victoria and New South Wales manhood suffrage, associated in the former case with the plural vote but not in the latter. In Victoria, the Conservatives, if I may so characterise the less-advanced party, have put forward a proposal which is unique in Australasia. They suggest that, while each man should continue to have a vote, the present plural votes should be replaced by a second vote which

[1] *Australasian Review of Reviews*, September, 1896.

should be possessed equally by all freeholders whatever be the size and number of their properties.
They believe that they would thereby place the
power in the hands of the more stable elements of
the population, and that they are not unlikely to be
supported by the freeholders, who constitute nearly
two-thirds of the electors on the rolls for the
Assembly.

At present the Labour parties are engaged in
onslaughts upon the Legislative Councils with a
view to their ultimate abolition, but are prepared to
accept, as an instalment, any proposals which would
cripple their power. They concurred heartily with
the Bill introduced in 1896 by the Government of
New South Wales and rejected by the Council after
it had been passed by large majorities through the
Assembly, which provided for the reference to a
popular vote of matters in dispute between the two
Houses. Similar measures are also advocated by
the Governments of Victoria, South Australia, and
Tasmania ; while in New Zealand, it is proposed
that deadlocks shall be obviated by a joint session of
both Houses, which shall sit as one Chamber. It
may be that an Act of 1891 which, as will be seen,
tends to popularise the Legislative Council in New
Zealand will account for the less drastic character
of the solution put forward in that Province. It is
probable that it will become customary in Australasia to submit distinct issues to the electorate, on a
separate ballot-paper, at the time of a general elec-

tion. The Government of South Australia ascertained in this manner the popular wishes in regard to religious instruction in State schools, and the payment to denominational schools of a capitation grant for secular results ; and the recent " Alcoholic Liquors Sale Control Act " of New Zealand provides that Local Option polls shall be taken concurrently with the election of representatives. Under references similar to that in South Australia, it may be objected, Ministers may be supported on their general policy, but be required to introduce a measure to which they are opposed. Such a position, however, would not apparently be regarded as inconsistent, as most of the candidates in South Australia stated their willingness to give effect to the popular vote, in whatever direction it might be expressed. Disputes between the two Houses will, I believe, be decided similarly, on the score of the expense of a special poll, unless the issue be such as to demand an immediate settlement.

The first line of attack of the Labour Members is thus seen to be an agitation which aims at enabling the electorate of the Assembly to override the Council ; the second is directed at its Conservative tendencies. The policy pursued depends upon the constitution of the Council : if it is elective, it should be so modified as to become a Chamber of paid representatives, subject to no property qualification and elected upon a wide franchise, such as the South Australian Council, in which a combination of Ministerialists and Labour Members has been able to obtain a bare majority. If it is nominated, the life tenure should be superseded by nomination for a short term of years, which will enable successive Ministries to introduce a new leaven of persons who are in touch with popular feeling, and will be prevented, by the limit placed upon the duration of their appointments, from being subjected to reactionary influences. The Council, that is to say, is to become a mere machine for registering the wishes of the Assembly. The only success which has hitherto attended this agitation is the enactment in 1891 of a measure in New Zealand which limited to seven years the duration of subsequent appointments ; but the Government now desire to abolish the life tenure, and they are followed herein by New South Wales, by providing for the gradual retirement of all the members who hold their seats for life. They also propose, whether seriously or in order to cast ridicule upon the Council, that women shall be eligible for appointment to that body. In regard to the general position of the nominated Councils, which are not limited as to the number of their members, it may be stated that the Imperial Government decided, upon a case submitted to them from New Zealand, that the Governor should accept the recommendations of his constitutional advisers in the matter of additional appointments. Strangely enough, the Premier of Queensland, the only other Australasian Province that has a nominated Legisla-

tive Council, though a strong constitutionalist, aimed
a blow at its prestige in a proposal, which he carried
through the Assembly but not through the Council,
that the former House alone should be vested with
the power of selecting the delegates to the pending
Federal Convention.

Before leaving this portion of the subject, I must
mention that other proposals affecting the form of
Government of the Provinces have been discussed
in Parliament and are likely to attract serious attention.   Theoretically, indeed, it has been asserted,
apart from the question of the power of the Upper
Houses, and the point is of interest as showing the
ideas germinating in the minds of Australasian politicians, that five changes are required in order that
the Parliamentary machinery may be brought into
proper relations with the people : the election of
Ministers by the Assembly ; continuity of representation in the Assembly, to be secured by the division
of the country into constituencies returning two
representatives who retire alternately at fixed periods ;
the Swiss form of Initiative and Referendum ; and
the right of a certain proportion of the members to
convoke a special session of Parliament, and of an
absolute majority of the electors in a constituency
to require the resignation of their member.   The
first and second of these reforms, as I have shown,
are included in the programme of the Ministry of
South Australia, which, however, in spite of its
success at the polls, has not pressed them forward

during the first session of the New Parliament. Continuity of representation could easily be arranged, as all the constituencies return two members. An Elective Executive Bill has been introduced in the House of Representatives in New Zealand and received a large measure of support, though it was opposed by the Premier and the leader of the Opposition. The idea has taken a strong hold upon the imagination of the Labour Members in all the Provinces.

It may be thought that I have laid stress upon a variety of fantastic theories, but the objection takes insufficient account of the facility with which changes can be effected in the absence of a strong force of traditional conservatism. I must admit, as a failing of Australasian politicians, that they are inclined to welcome innovations which are superficially attractive, without due consideration of the ulterior consequences. To quote an extreme case, the Government of New Zealand proposed, in a Single Bill, not only to abolish the life tenure of Members of the Legislative Council, but to provide machinery for the settlement of disputes between the two Houses and to establish a modified form of the Swiss Referendum. But I am confident that several of the proposals to which I have referred, notably that for an Elective Executive, meet with a large measure of support in the constituencies. This movement has gathered strength from the disinclination of Ministries to resign except upon a

direct vote of want of confidence. Some of them
look with equanimity upon the defeat of cardinal
principles of important Bills, whether it be due to
the strength of the Opposition or the defection of
their own followers, and do not hesitate, if sufficient
pressure be exercised, to withdraw them altogether.
As the Ministry tends, therefore, to become a body
which carries out the wishes of the whole House,
and ceases to lead its own Party, the position would
be simplified if the whole House elected the Executive for a fixed period. Another argument is found
in the increasing desire of the Assembly to shift its
legislative duties to the shoulders of the Executive.
Parliament decides the broad principles of measures
and leaves the details to be filled in by Regulations
made by the Department concerned under the
supervision of the Minister and with the approval of
the Executive Council.

(2) Graduated death duties are imposed in all
the seven Provinces, though in Tasmania the tax
levied on the largest properties does not exceed 3
per cent. Western Australia came into line with
the other Provinces in 1895, when a Bill imposing
graduation up to 10 per cent. was passed, almost
without discussion, through both Houses of Parliament. The Premier admitted that it had not been
rendered necessary by the condition of the finances,
but contended that it should be placed upon the
Statute Book while there were few rich men in the
community who would resent it.

Other forms of direct taxation are as follows : New Zealand, South Australia, and New South Wales have taxation on incomes and land values, the two former with, the latter without, graduation ; Victoria has a graduated income tax and an ungraduated land tax on estates above a certain value ; Tasmania, an ungraduated tax on incomes and the capital value of land ; Queensland, an ungraduated income tax, which is only collected on dividends paid by public companies. The taxation in New South Wales, Victoria, New Zealand, and South Australia has been promoted, if not inspired, by the Labour Movement in Parliament, and constitutes its greatest triumph. In Victoria the taxation of land values was rejected by the Legislative Council.

A point of interest is the distinction made by Victoria, Tasmania, and South Australia between incomes derived from property and those which are the result of personal exertion. It is thought to be equitable that the former should be taxed at a higher rate, and the principle is similar to that which dictates the taxation of land upon its un-improved value.

(3) I have referred very briefly in the present chapter to certain forms of industrial legislation ; speaking generally, they are based upon English examples and do not call for any particular com-ment. The Labour Parties are keenly interested in these matters because it is simpler, apart from greater efficacy, that inspectors should protect their

interest under Acts of Parliament than that they should be compelled constantly to engage in negotiations with individual employers.

(4) As I have already pointed out, the consideration of Australasian problems must be accompanied by a recollection of the difference of conditions from those existing in Great Britain. Even in the latter country it is obvious that the intimate relations between employers and employed are being replaced, especially in the manufacturing centres, by a purely monetary bond; but they can never, except in individual cases, have had any existence in Australasia, where capitalists and workmen have approached each other and entered into agreements as strangers. Consequently the workmen, attached neither to people nor places, have been prepared to move as their varying interests have suggested and have formed few lasting ties with their employers. Many of the industries, indeed, have tended to accentuate this absence of cordial relations: in pastoralism, for instance, the small permanent staff is supplemented for a few weeks in the year by a large number of shearers and others, who sign a definite agreement with their employers, and, provided that the conditions are carried out, can have no interest either in them or in their properties. Incidentally, an association recently formed at Sydney which engages shearers and provides them with consecutive employment at different sheds, should not only be a financial success, but allay the

natural dissatisfaction of a body of men who, though they earn high wages, can depend upon neither regularity nor permanency in their work. I could show that similar conditions prevail in the sugar industry and, to some extent, in agriculture ; but enough has been said to prove that the working classes are differently situated from those in older countries and partially to explain their willingness to form themselves into Trades Unions and the combativeness of these organisations.

The great maritime strike, though it has been followed by the Broken Hill strikes of 1891 and 1892, the shearers' strikes of 1891 and 1894, and periodical hostilities at Newcastle, has modified largely the attitude of the working classes in regard to the efficacy of industrial warfare. The later struggles have principally affected Queensland and New South Wales, which was the first of the Provinces to attempt to deal with the matter by Act of Parliament. A Board of Conciliation was established upon the recommendation of a Royal Commission, but is admitted to have been a failure in the absence of any compulsory reference of disputes. On the occasion of the most recent disturbances, at Newcastle in 1896, which originated upon an application of the miners for higher wages, the Premier, following English precedents, intervened, and was enabled to settle the dispute, though not until the strike had lasted for three months and had caused much of the foreign trade to be diverted to foreign ports. Actual

and prospective losses caused the owners, though
they made a small concession at the request of the
Premier, to refuse to reinstate the miners except at a
slightly lower rate of wages than that against which
they had struck. The offer, as modified by the
Premier, was accepted by the miners, who had thus,
at the cost of much misery, brought about a reduction in their wages. The disturbances of 1894 in
Queensland, which reached an acute stage, were
met by the Government by resolute administration
under special powers obtained by Act of Parliament,
but no attempt was made to intervene between the
disputants or to make use of the Conciliation Act of
1892, which, as far as I know, has remained a dead
letter. It is useless, therefore, to discuss the Act
further than to say that its machinery can only be
set in motion by a Local Authority, but it may not
be unfair to attribute the unsympathetic attitude of
the Government to the bitterness engendered by the
extravagances of the Labour Party.

In most of the Provinces neither the employers
nor the workmen are prepared, as yet, to bind themselves to refer their disputes to an impartial tribunal
and to abide by its decision. Though the tendency
in that direction is on the increase, it has been
suggested that, in the meanwhile, Boards should be
constituted which would be empowered to consider
disputes, and, after the examination of books and
witnesses, to issue a public report. The judgment
would not be enforceable, but might be expected, in

the majority of cases, to lead to a settlement of the difficulty; at any rate, it would influence public opinion, which is a large factor in all industrial struggles. But South Australia and New Zealand have passed this stage, and have placed drastic measures on their Statute Book which provide, in certain cases, for compulsory awards. The compulsory provisions of the South Australian Act apply only to employers and workmen who are organised and have voluntarily accepted them by the process of registration. Should they become involved in an industrial dispute, the Governor may, upon the recommendation of the President of the State Board of Conciliation, cause the matter to be referred to it, and the Board may make an award which will be binding upon the parties concerned. In New Zealand, on the other hand, while the proceedings must be initiated by employers or workmen who are registered, the other party, though unregistered, may be called upon, should the Board of Conciliation fail to effect a settlement, to attend before the Court of Arbitration and to obey its award, subject to the general proviso that an employer may suspend or discontinue any industry and an employé cease from working therein. In neither Province is a strike or lock-out permitted during the deliberations of the tribunal.

The Acts do not apply to unorganised workers, except indirectly, partly because they have not been the cause of the great industrial struggles of the past, partly because it would be difficult, if not impossible, to enforce awards against them. It may also have been thought that they would be encouraged thereby to form themselves into Unions, and that the best chance of industrial peace lies in negotiations between responsible bodies of workers and employers who will have too much at stake to be willing to proceed thoughtlessly to extremities. As regards registration, it has been found that the workers of South Australia, though their leaders had supported the compulsory provisions, have been backward in this direction ; but that, in New Zealand, no such hesitation has been displayed. The workers in that country do not appear to share the disinclination to agree to the intervention of an arbitrator which is stated to be increasing in Great Britain.

In South Australia, to give a brief account of the new tribunals, Boards of Conciliation may be either Private Boards, constituted under industrial agreements and endowed with such jurisdiction as may be confided to them in the agreements ; or Public Boards, which include Local Boards constituted for particular localities and particular industries, and the State Board of Conciliation. In New Zealand, the first reference is to an elective Board of Conciliation constituted for the district in which the dispute has occurred. Should it fail to effect a settlement, the matter may be referred to the Court of Arbitration, which, similarly with the State Board

of Conciliation in South Australia, consists of an
equal number of representatives of employers and
employed and a chairman nominated by the Government, who must, in the former country, be a judge
of the Supreme Court. These tribunals are invested
with full powers to require the attendance and
examination of witnesses, and may either make an
award which shall take effect for a period not
exceeding two years, and may be enforced by legal
process against associations and individuals, or they
may confine themselves, at their discretion, to a
recommendation which will be merely a direction
to the parties concerned.

In South Australia the State Board has also the
power to inquire into, and report upon, industrial
disputes, though the parties be not registered. This
portion of the Act has alone been brought into
operation, and that unsuccessfully, as, though the
representatives of employers and employed on the
Board arrived at a unanimous decision upon a dispute affecting the rate of wages, the employer in
question refused to be guided by its judgment. The
general failure of the Act, though the affirmation
of the principle of Conciliation has been valuable,
has been due partly to the absence of serious disputes in South Australia, but principally to the
unwillingness both of employers and employed to
place themselves in a position in which they will
lose control over the terms of employment.

The Act passed by the Government of New

Zealand, on the contrary, has hitherto been entirely efficacious, and has prevented the interruption of harmonious relations between employers and employed. It was first tested upon a dispute which arose over the action of the Consolidated Goldfields Company in reducing wages in the mines from 10s. to 8s. 4d. per day. The men, who were not members of a union, went out on strike, and were then offered wages at the rate of 9s. Upon the advice of their leaders, the men accepted the offer provisionally; and, having formed themselves into a union which they promptly caused to be registered, referred the matter to the Board of Conciliation. The decision of the Board, which it is unnecessary to specify, was refused by the men, who appealed to the Court of Arbitration. The award of the latter body, which fixed the wages of miners at 9s. 6d. per day, a rate smaller than that which had been received by the men, but larger than that against which they had protested, has been observed loyally by the Company and its employés.

The next dispute arose at Christchurch upon the expiration of the agreement which had been in operation between the boot manufacturers and their workmen for several years, and upon the desire of the former to substitute new terms which were regarded as distasteful. It was concerned with several matters of detail, but hinged principally upon the question whether non-unionists should be allowed to work with unionists. As in the former case, an appeal was made from the Board of Conciliation's award to the Court of Arbitration, whose decision, it is noteworthy, both sides had signified their willingness to accept. The award applied to all the bootmakers in the Province with the exception of three or four who were not identified with the boot manufacturers' association, and was accompanied by remarks pronounced, it must be remembered, by a judge of the Supreme Court, which cannot fail to be of interest to the Trades Unionists in all parts of the world. I do not, therefore, apologise for quoting them at length :—

"The Arbitration Court has not hitherto been in the habit of giving reasons for its decision. It appears to the Court that, sitting as arbitrators, it should as a general rule follow the ordinary practice of arbitrators and simply give its decision without reasons. In the present case, however, so far as I myself am concerned, I think it is desirable that I should, with respect to part of the award, give some indications of the reasons which have induced the Court to arrive at its conclusion. The part of the award to which I refer is that which relates to clauses 1 and 2 of the general rules which the Manufacturers' Association has submitted to the Court : '1. (*a*) It is the individual right of the employer to decide whom he shall employ or dismiss. (*b*) It is the individual right of the workman to accept or refuse work from any employer.

2. Employers or employés, either individually or
through any organisation, shall not discriminate for
or against any person because he is or is not a
member of any organisation, neither shall there be
any distinction between organised or non-organised
labour ; both shall work under the same conditions
and receive equal pay for equal work.' The Bootmakers' Union, in opposition to the rules so suggested, put forward the contention that employment
should be limited to members of the Bootmakers'
Union. The Court, however, is not able to accept
the extreme view which has been put forward by
the Bootmakers' Union. If it were accepted it
might follow that an employer, who had work to
do and who could not get Union men to do it,
might have to bring his operations to a standstill.
The effect of it also would be that non-Union men
would be absolutely prevented from earning their
living in the workshops of the members of the
Manufacturers' Association. That, so far as I am
concerned, seems to be going beyond what the
Court ought to decree. On the other hand, however, I am not prepared to accept absolutely clauses
1 and 2 in the form in which the Manufacturers'
Association has put them forward. The Court
ought, I think, to comply with the intention of
the Legislature as evidenced in the provisions of
the Industrial Conciliation and Arbitration Act, and
ought not to do anything which is calculated to
destroy or weaken any industrial organisation. The

intention of the Act is indicated in its title—the Act is an Act to encourage the formation of Industrial Unions and Associations. The Court, therefore, ought not to do anything which will tend to destroy or weaken an industrial association, or interfere with the manifest intention of the Legislature as disclosed by the Act. We have this also, that for the last three years the shops of the Manufacturers' Association have been practically working as Union shops. It is true that manufacturers say—probably with truth—that they were so worked because they could not help it, but the fact remains that they have been working in that way, and the proposed new rules, as put forward by the manufacturers, expressly reverse the previous mode of working. We have this also, that the previous statement was a statement agreed to between the Manufacturers' Association and the Bootmakers' Union, the conference which followed the statement was between the Association and the Union, and the dispute now before the Court is between the Association and the Union. It is only by means of Unions that labour can take advantage of the Act. Under these circumstances, it seems to me not unreasonable that the Union should stipulate for special privileges to its members. The Union are fighting the battle, and it is fair that they should say that the results of the victory, so far as it is a victory, and has any beneficial results, should accrue to them, at any rate in the first instance. They fight

the battle for their members, and not for the sake
of outside labour. Under these circumstances it
appears to me that it is quite reasonable that the
members of the Union should have preference in
employment ; that members of the Union who are
competent should not have to wait about while
non-members of the Union are employed in the
shops of the Boot Manufacturers' Association. The
Court, therefore, has modified Rules 1 and 2 in this
direction. I need hardly say that each case to be
decided under this Act must depend on the particular circumstances attaching to it ; that no one
case can be treated as a precedent to any future
case, and that because under the particular circumstances of a particular case, this Court has decided
as it has decided, that is no reason why, under
different or varying circumstances, a similar decision
ought to be come to. The Court in coming to its
decision, takes into consideration not general principles so much as the special circumstances of each
particular case."

The award, which modified the regulations on the
lines laid down by the Court, is regarded as a great
triumph by Trade Unionists, who are, not unnaturally, inclined to apply it as a precedent to all
organised trades.

A possible exemplification of the efficacy of the
Act occurred at the end of 1896, when the engineers
employed in the Australian trade of the Union
Steamship Company of New Zealand asked that

their wages might be raised to the rate which had prevailed before the financial troubles. They took advantage of the increased traffic caused by the holidays in order to emphasise their demands. The engineers of the ships plying in New Zealand waters made a similar request, which was at once acceded to by the Company, but did not attempt to exert undue pressure. I am not prepared to state that the difference in attitude was due to the Conciliation and Arbitration Act of the latter country, but the coincidence is calculated to encourage that belief. The Managing Director of the Company (Mr. James Mills) told me that he was a hearty supporter of compulsion, not so much because he believed in arbitration, as because a strike or lock-out was obviated, and the parties to a dispute, often trivial at the outset, were brought together before they had been embittered by mutual recriminations. Mr. Kingston, the Premier of South Australia, and the principal promoter of the South Australian Act, has written in a similar strain :—

"Conciliation Boards should be established in anticipation of the differences they are designed to prevent. On the occasion of a great strike, the public cries out for conciliation. Suggestions are received from all quarters recommending Conferences and Arbitration ; but when war has been declared, and the disputants, as it were, are at each other's throats, each hopeful of ultimate success, they are seldom in the mood to listen to peacemakers. If either party fears the result of the contest, it may favour pacific counsels. There is, however, a vehement probability that the stronger party will reject all overtures and insist on an unconditional surrender and all the advantages which victory can command. The dispute is then determined, not on its merits, but by sheer strength. The vanquished, smarting under a sense of defeat and injustice, capitulate only with the view to the early renewal of the struggle under more favourable circumstances." [1]

(5) A large proportion of the workmen of Australasia are convinced believers in Protection in the widest sense of the word. As far as their opinion can be ascertained from the representation of Labour in Parliament, it is unanimous in Victoria, South Australia, and New Zealand. In New South Wales, as has been seen, the Labour Members have, for the sake of solidarity, sunk the fiscal issue; but the majority are Protectionists, and have proposed that the question of the tariff should be settled for a fixed period by a plebiscite. Thereby they believe that they will secure Protection and continue to be unfettered in their support of the more advanced party. In Queensland, also, the Labour programme states that the fiscal issue is not to be regarded as a party question.

Protection, the Labour Members admit, raises prices to the consumer; but they contend that, if prices are high, employers can afford to pay high

---

[1] *Australasian Review of Reviews*, August 20, 1894.

wages, and that the strength of Trades Unionism
should be sufficient to enforce them. To put their
argument, such as it is, in a nutshell, it is better to
have high prices and high wages than low prices
combined with low wages and uncertain employment. Then, as combination is expected to keep
wages at a high point, it is obvious that it can be
exercised most effectually over a small area, and we
find the South Australian Labour Members voting
against a resolution in favour of inter-provincial
Free Trade, and Labour Members generally imbued
with an actual, if not avowed, opposition to Federation, the first result of which would, it is believed,
be the removal of fiscal barriers. They profess,
indeed, a desire for Federation on a democratic
basis, but are, as far as their material interests are
concerned, under the influence of a patriotism which
is intensely provincial and does not take account of
national, much less of imperial, considerations.

If he lives under a protective tariff, the workman
asks himself of what use is it to exclude the products
of cheap labour if the cheap labourer be allowed to
enter the country and compete with him on the
spot. The agitation against Asiatic immigrants has,
I am prepared to admit, a wider basis, and rests
largely upon physical repugnance and the fear that
they might enter in such large numbers as to swamp
the white population. To that extent it appeals to
the Free Traders of New South Wales, who have
not been backward in their support of anti-Chinese

legislation, and meets with the general support of
Australians, as was shown by the unanimity with
which the Premiers, assembled in Conference early
in 1896, decided against participation in the Anglo-
Japanese treaty and in favour of the extension to
other coloured races of the restrictions placed upon
the influx of the Chinese. But, from the point
of view of the working classes, antipathy is felt,
principally, towards competitors who have a lower
standard of comfort, and the difficulties placed in
the way of Imperial statesmanship are persistently
ignored.

Thence, by an easy transition of thought, the
objection is extended to all labourers whose competition, through the stress of necessity, may tend to
reduce wages. The indigent Italian or German is
equally undesirable, as are indigent Englishmen, who
alone, among Europeans, are likely to arrive in large
numbers. Some of them, it is known, have been
assisted to emigrate, by philanthropic agencies or
otherwise, because they were unable to earn a livelihood at home. South Australia, Victoria, Tasmania,
and New Zealand seek to exclude paupers by the
provision that the owner or master of a ship bringing persons who are likely to become a charge upon
the public or any charitable institution, may be
called upon to execute a bond to pay all expenses
incurred within five years for the maintenance or
support of such persons. But the workman reserves his strongest condemnation for the proposal

that he should be compelled to contribute, through taxation or Custom duties, to State-aided immigration, which increases the number of his competitors. Herein is seen the cloven foot of the capitalist, which must be concealed, except in Queensland, where capital and labour are in open antagonism and the former is at present in the ascendant.

The ultimate development of protective ideas is found in the annual tax levied on foreign commercial travellers in New Zealand and in the desire to subject immigrants to physical as well as pecuniary and racial tests. In New Zealand the Undesirable Immigrants Exclusion Bill, and the equally unsuccessful Public Health Bill of 1896, forbade masters of ships, under a heavy penalty, to introduce persons who are consumptive into the Provinces. Consumption, it is known, has proved deadly to the Maoris, and, to an even greater extent, to half-castes.

It is not my intention to discuss the wisdom of the measures by which Australians seek to keep out Asiatics, indigent Europeans, criminals, and persons in ill-health. The Imperial Government, of course, can have no objection to the imposition of pecuniary disqualifications which, being of general application, do not conflict with treaty obligations, though the policy is diametrically opposed to that which has prevailed hitherto in England. I merely wish to point out the strength of Australasian opposition to unrestricted competition, and to express considerable sympathy with workmen who, having seen, or having learnt from their parents, how much misery and pauperism are to be found in older countries, are inhospitable to strangers and will do all in their power to prevent a fall to a similar level. Many of them have noted the existence of destitution in Sydney and Melbourne, and dread the operation of any cause which would be likely to intensify it.

It cannot be denied that, as England is the principal competitor with native manufactures, and the only European country from which immigration on a large scale is likely to arise, some of the working men entertain a feeling of hostility towards the Mother Country. Ill-feeling is also promoted by the condition of financial dependence. Australians are inclined to complain, however unreasonably, that, had it not been for the temptations to which they were exposed by British capitalists, their Provinces could not have incurred the extravagant expenditure under which they are suffering and must continue to suffer. Australia, it has been said, owes to England merely the gratitude of the poor man toward his pawnbroker. I should not have mentioned the existence of these views, which are confined to a small section of the community, were it not that they seem ominous for the future, when we remember the principal cause of the estrangement between the Eastern and Western States of America. In spite of inquiries and

observation, I have been unable to form an opinion
as to the general attitude, which is being modified
year by year by the increase in the proportion of
native-born Australians. At one extreme of the
social scale are those who bask in the sunshine of
titled vice-royalty, at the other those in whom the
continual struggle for existence precludes the possibility of national, not to mention Imperial, ideals.
The large intermediate classes, which will control
the future, appear to be animated by great sympathy
with the English people. I am led to believe that
the boisterous loyalty of the past has been replaced
by a deeper feeling of kinship, which was displayed
in marked fashion on the occasion of the German
Emperor's telegram after the Transvaal raid. On
the other hand, the growing independence of a
young nation and the sentimental, but none the
less real, objection to the term " Colonial," which is
regarded as a mark of inferiority, have convinced
some Imperialistic Australians that the shortest road
to Federation lies through separation. Others, I
have been surprised to note, do not consider that
permanence of friendly relations necessarily implies
continuance under one flag. Englishmen will be
disappointed to learn that there is little general
appreciation, especially among native-born Australians, of the benefits accruing from the protection
of the British fleet. Never having known the
horrors of war and removed from the area of
great armaments, they are not aware of the dangers

against which they are guarded. In fact, many of them grudge the "contributions without representation" that are given towards the maintenance of the Australian squadron. In foreign politics Australians are strongly Imperialistic, and will respect Great Britain as long as she maintains the dignity of her position. In domestic affairs they resent the interference of the Colonial Office, rarely though it be exercised, and do not take sufficient account of international difficulties. They are satisfied, moreover, with existing conditions, and do not manifest any desire for closer union with Great Britain at present, though any proposals emanating from the Imperial Government will be received with respectful attention and may meet with theoretical approval ; and, while the recent Presidential election in the United States convinced them of the disadvantages of Republican institutions, they are prepared to wait upon the natural evolution of events, and believe that, in the meanwhile, we should strive, through the press, travel, and otherwise, to become better acquainted with each other's ideas and aspirations, and to correct many of the wrong impressions which prevail both in Australia and Great Britain. This policy is not heroic but practical, especially if it could be accompanied by a greater identification of Australia with the Empire. If a few hundred Australians could be recruited, in spite of the lowness of the pay, for service in the Army and Navy, they would, I am convinced, upon their return, do much to broaden the minds of their countrymen. Australia and New Zealand, it must be remembered, are isolated from the rest of the world. Again, some of the vacancies in the Indian Civil Service might be filled by examinations held in Australia simultaneously with those in England. These suggestions, which could be amplified and extended by men of greater experience, may be regarded as trivial and unimportant, but I am confident that they indicate the direction in which Englishmen can most effectually seek to retain the affections of their Australasian kinsfolk. The problems of Australian Federation will tax all the resources of statesmanship, and must, in my opinion, be solved before there can be any profitable discussion of modified and closer relations with the Mother Country. It seems to me that the Victorian or Queenslander must realise that he is an Australian before he can be expected to appreciate the meaning of the words, " Civis Britannicus Sum."

The subject of Australian Federation has been discussed at length in a preceding chapter. I need only point out that politicians are bound to recognise three lines of severance : the artificial boundaries between one Province and another, the diversity of opinions engendered by differences of climate, as exemplified principally in the attitude in regard to Polynesian labour, and the divergence of development between the denizens of towns and the more settled areas and those who are struggling against the inclemencies of nature in the back country. I felt, and others have chronicled a similar impression, that I had entered into a different country when I travelled in the Western Downs of Queensland. I found myself, if I may generalise from a limited experience of shearers, among a class of men who are thoroughly honest but absolutely narrow-minded and interested only in matters which concern their means of livelihood. They form their opinions from an advanced organ of labour, which is their principal, if not only, literature, and even such of them as are emigrants from Great Britain have little knowledge of the leading events of recent years.

The urban population, of course, is in a different position, and is kept by the newspapers in touch with local and Imperial affairs. Apart from the causes of the aggregation of large centres which have been discussed in the opening pages of this chapter, and may be supplemented by the observations of Sir Charles Dilke,[1] it may be noted, as a subsidiary influence, that a high standard of comfort makes people unwilling to face the hardship of the bush, that squatters are inclined to place their sons in urban professions, and that education turns out clerks rather than manual labourers. But the dwellers in towns are, on the whole, comfortably situated; even Melbourne and Sydney do not

---

[1] "Problems of Greater Britain," vol. ii. pp. 246–8.

show an average of more than 2·73 and 4·87 persons to the acre ; but these figures include the suburbs, and must be amended if the metropolis proper is solely regarded.

But, in spite of this consideration, the working classes of Australasia have little to complain of. Destitution exists, as is inevitable under present conditions, but many workers, especially in Victoria, are owners of their homes, and all the younger men have had the benefit of a general system of national education and of the favourable situation of their class. This is due partly to the position attained, and not subsequently lost, when the rush of men to the goldfields produced a scarcity of labour ; partly to the fact which has already been noted, that the men who emigrated from Great Britain were imbued with the spirit which qualified them to assert themselves. Hitherto they have not proved themselves unworthy of their nationality. They are uniformly courteous, in my experience, to those who are civil to them, and do not expect the servility of older countries, and are the most law-abiding people in the world. On a Saturday night in Coolgardie I found things to be as quiet as in a small country town in England. The larrikinism of Melbourne and Sydney has been much exaggerated, and does not extend beyond the capitals ; in the former city, at the annual festival which marks the recurrence of the Melbourne Cup, the behaviour of the crowd is such

as would be a credit to any country. But Australians and New Zealanders, as any visitor cannot
but note, take their pleasures sadly, and have
transplanted the seriousness of a Northern land
to a climate which should lend itself to merriment
and laughter. How far their character has been
modified I am not prepared to say : on the one
hand, employment is not subject to seasonal
interruptions ; on the other, the pressure of cold
upon industry is entirely wanting. The climate
has, however, in spite of the denunciations of the
Prohibitionists, undoubtedly conduced to temperate
habits. Time after time did I notice, during my
travels, that all the company were drinking tea,
and I have been assured that shearers and other
labourers no longer waste their earnings upon
drink. The temperance of the younger generation has also been promoted by the spread of
education and by the love of athletics ; which
necessitates physical soundness. Speaking generally and responsibly, the working classes, which
form the backbone of every country, though they
pay high rent, earn high wages, and, as they do
not pay high prices for their food or clothing,
are enabled to become self - respecting members
of a self-respecting community.

XI

A VISIT TO THE COOLGARDIE GOLDFIELDS IN MARCH, 1896.

I SAILED from Marseilles for Australia by one of the large steamers of the Messageries Maritimes Company. Among my fellow travellers was a mining expert, bound for the Western Australian goldfields, who proposed that I should accompany him, and said that, as he knew the leading people on the fields, he would be able to render my trip agreeable. I gladly accepted his offer, and have since had cause to consider that I was most fortunate, as I believe that some such introduction as mine is indispensable.

The large mail steamers all touch Western Australia at Albany, distant 340 miles from Perth and 570 miles from Coolgardie. The Government are carrying out very extensive harbour works at Fremantle, the port of Perth, in the hope of inducing the mail steamers to call there, and they believe that, when a railway line has been constructed between

Perth and Adelaide, a line which must eventually be built, though perhaps not for many years, Fremantle will become a place of great importance, as, beyond being the shipping port for the produce of the Coolgardie goldfields, it will be the point of arrival and departure of the mails between Great Britain and all the Australian Provinces.

We reached Albany, which is 200 miles further from Coolgardie than Fremantle, late in the evening, and, having missed by a few hours the direct train which runs three times a week to Perth, we spent the night at a third-rate hotel, unable to sleep owing to the attacks of the mosquitoes, and left by train the next morning after a breakfast consisting of coarse meat and impossible eggs. We soon lost sight of the bay of Albany, and, plunging into the bush, travelled through it the whole day. The heat was overpowering, as we were still almost at the height of summer. In the afternoon a stranger came into the compartment and enlivened us with anecdotes of his experiences at an outlying station. In several stories he referred to actions which showed him to have behaved in the most ruthlessly cruel manner towards the aborigines. To quote one among many : A young native servant in his employment came to believe that, owing to some unintentional contravention of the religious observances of his people, he was doomed to die within three days ; so he lay on his back and refused to take food. As he was a good workman, his master first tried to induce him to rise, then thrashed him with all his might, and afterwards had him dragged along the ground by his hair until he was so exhausted that he came unconscious. It is needless to add that, on his recovery, the man had been cured of his obstinacy. Such conduct, I am convinced, is most exceptional. All the Australasian Governments are actuated by a sincere desire to protect the aborigines, as are the vast majority of the inhabitants. But, as long as many districts are sparsely settled, isolated cases of barbarous cruelty must continue to occur.

After thirteen hours of travel we reached Beverley, where we were obliged to spend the night, and again suffered from bad accommodation, indifferent food, and mosquitoes. A journey of five hours on the following morning took us to Perth, where we proposed to spend a few days. My companion noticed a great difference in the appearance of the town ; a few years ago, he told me, it was lifeless and dull, strangers rarely arrived, trade was stagnant, and the whole place wore an air of listlessness. The rapid change must be put down entirely to the success of the goldfields, even allowing full credit to the Government for their efforts to develop all the resources of the country. The population of the Province has doubled during the last five years ; the population of Perth has more than doubled, and large business firms have established branches there. But great though its progress has been, it is hard to realise that this place, which is not larger than an English country town, is the capital and seat of government of a Province of nearly a million square miles, which possesses 1,200 miles of railway and goldfields of enormous extent, which seem likely to take rank among the most productive of the world. Perth is picturesquely situated on the Swan River, and should increase largely beyond its present dimensions. Handsome brick buildings alternate even in the principal thoroughfares with miserable shanties which are bound soon to disappear. In the evening the streets present a scene of great animation, as hundreds of people may be seen walking up and down, eagerly discussing the mining news, which always presents some feature of interest. Men gather together in small groups, whispering weighty secrets which may or may not be intended for the benefit of their hearers, for in Perth, as elsewhere, we hear that large fortunes have been made through the credulity and folly of the too eager investor.

At Perth I made several purchases, all of which were of use to me : a pair of dark blue spectacles with perforated sides, as a protection against the dust and sun, a fly-net and a water-bag. The latter, made of canvas, in order that its contents may be cooled by evaporation, is carried by all travellers who distrust the quality of the water which they are likely to obtain at wayside stations.

At the time of my visit to the goldfields, the

railway terminated at Bullabulling, some eighteen miles from Coolgardie. The journey from Perth to Coolgardie was a matter of twenty-eight hours. Leaving in the afternoon, we arrived the next morning at Southern Cross, the centre of a mining district which has been eclipsed by those further east. We had breakfast at an unpretentious little hotel, the landlady of which harrowed us by accounts of the amount of typhoid fever prevalent in the place. Her own servant was ill, several deaths had recently occurred, and she had heard the undertaker in the early morning again at work upon a coffin. We continued our journey by the contractor's train, covering one hundred miles in seven hours and passing through scenery which became terribly wearisome from its dreary monotony. So far we had travelled comfortably enough, but the last eighteen miles by coach were more tiring than the whole of the rest of the journey. The road was inches deep in dust and full of holes, and we ploughed our way along it at the rate of five miles an hour, a pace which was not maintained when darkness set in and the driver could no longer pick his way in the best track, but continually jolted us in the deep ruts and bumped the coach against tree stumps. Upon our arrival at Coolgardie, we found a difficulty in obtaining rooms; at the principal hotel no accommodation of any kind was to be had ; at another all the rooms were occupied, but we were offered a shake-down which we thought it wise to accept. We learnt the next day that twenty-three extra beds had been made up, in the drawing-room, on the balcony, in fact at every available spot, and that the rush had continued for more than a year.

The following morning I looked out upon a sandy track which represents the main street of Coolgardie. It was already a scene of some animation ; camels, driven by Afghans, were carrying their heavy burdens in and out of the town ; aborigines, with their wives and children, in all their degraded ugliness, were passing to and fro ; and bustling merchants and clerks were hurrying past on bicycles to their various occupations. The houses of Coolgardie are built of a framework of wood, covered with a sheeting of galvanised iron. The town is entirely dependent for all its supplies on the outside world, as the country, within a radius of at least one hundred miles, will produce food for neither man nor beast. The question of water supply, even for domestic purposes, was until recently a great difficulty ; but several fresh water wells have been sunk which, together with the output of numerous condensers, give an ample supply for the town. The rainfall is very small, and too irregular to be depended upon. The sky is often overcast for weeks and rain threatens daily, but the clouds gradually disperse and leave the land as parched as before.

Strolling out of the town we found ourselves

on the outskirts of a mining district. As far as the eye could see, the country was studded with tents, mining shafts, and condensers, and the soil was everywhere raised in irregular heaps. For miles around every sod of earth has been turned over and put through a blower in the search for the alluvial gold which has been found there in great quantities. We came upon an old man who said that the land upon which he was working had not been thoroughly sifted, and showed us a few grains of gold which he had obtained as the result of his labours. A little further on we came to some mines, and my companion pointed out and explained to me the machinery by which the gold is separated from the stone. A return of an ounce of gold to a ton of quartz is, speaking generally, regarded as satisfactory, but many other factors have to be weighed in the consideration of the question whether a mine is likely to repay the outlay upon it, such as the width and probable extent of the reef, and the possibility of obtaining an adequate amount of water for working the machinery. I gathered that there could be no doubt as to the richness of the reefs on several of the goldfields of Western Australia, but that, on most of them, the great difficulty has been, and still is, the inadequacy of the water supply.

We did not remain long at Coolgardie, but continued our journey to Kalgoorlie, a small township twenty-four miles from Coolgardie and the centre of the field where my companion had to do most of his work as a mining expert. We travelled by coach in the early morning and had a further experience of the discomforts of a rough and heavy track. Kalgoorlie was a repetition of Coolgardie, on a smaller scale. Both are the creation of the last few years and must not be judged by too high a standard. The town authorities have done their best to procure good sanitary conditions and have been aided by the Government, who give, as a subsidy to municipalities, one pound for every pound raised from general rates, and have also assisted them in the erection and maintenance of hospitals ; but the lack of funds has retarded improvements which the authorities have been anxious to carry out. We arrived at Kalgoorlie on a Sunday, and noticed that the inhabitants, most of whom are adults, bachelors or married men separated from their wives and families, were loitering about with every appearance of utter boredom.

From the town we walked to one of the neighbouring camps where my companion had acquaintances. These camps offer a much pleasanter life than that in the towns. Each forms in itself a small settlement of large canvas tents fitted up by the residents, who have a common mess and every opportunity of leading a sociable life. At the camp which we visited we found several of the men disporting themselves in hammocks in an arbour made of closely plaited branches of trees, which kept off the heat of the sun and admitted a cool current of air. In the course of conversation it was arranged that we should visit several of the mines on the following day.

In the morning we visited a mine upon which little had, so far, been done. We were placed at the top of the shaft in a small cage, by which we were let down to a depth of a hundred feet. Then we were led along a labyrinth of passages from which my companions gathered the direction and extent of the reef, and we were shown various points at which the gold, which was of a coarse character, could clearly be seen in the stone. In the afternoon we visited another mine which was of more interest to me. A shaft had been sunk to a depth of two hundred feet, at which level water had been struck, and the miners were busily at work. Again we were let down in a cage, and wandered through seemingly endless passages, which reminded me, in my ignorance, of parts of the catacombs at Rome, as nothing appeared to the unsophisticated eye but the bare rock. The gold was very fine, and only visible to us when the foreman struck off a flake and pointed it out to us glistening in minute particles in the quartz. He told me that ordinary miners earned £3 10s. a week, those working in the water at the low level £4, but that they could not live on less than £2, and, even so, only in the roughest way. The life is, however, not an unhealthy one, as the mines are, to judge from those that I visited, well ventilated. The mine and other surrounding properties have created a thriving settlement; well-built offices have been erected, hundreds of men are employed, and the ear is continually greeted by the din of machinery. In the evening we returned to Kalgoorlie and heard, near our hotel, a service held by the Salvation Army in the centre of the street. A large group of loungers stood around, moved neither to ribaldry nor attention, but apparently listening in complete indifference to the ipassionate pleadings of the preachers. Some yards away a mining agent was doing a brisk business in shares.

A few days later I retraced my steps to Coolgardie, and thence to Perth. On the homeward journey I had experiences of much discomfort. On the coach between Coolgardie and Bullabulling, I managed, as on the previous occasion, by a private arrangement with the driver, to secure the box-seat, in order to be at an elevation from the dust. But the wind was behind us, and we were soon enveloped in such a cloud of dust that it was often impossible to see the leaders, and, as there is no rule of the road, we had narrow escapes of colliding with teams travelling in the opposite direction. Upon our arrival at Bullabulling, we found that the contractor's train contained only one passenger carriage, which was already crowded; so several of us climbed on an open luggage truck and made ourselves tolerably comfortable, though we suffered from the blazing heat of the mid-day sun. My neighbour was a man who had had a most varied career. In his youth he had managed a small hosiery shop in an English Midland town ; then, as his health was bad, he had emigrated to Victoria, where he had unsuccessfully carried on grazing operations. He had been attracted to Western Australia by the discoveries of gold, and had bought a waggon and team of horses, with which he had carried goods between Southern Cross and Coolgardie before the construction of the railway. He told me that the life had been very hard, and pointed out to me portions of the road which were so heavy that a progress of ten miles was regarded as a satisfactory day's work. He was then on his way to revisit the "old country," after an absence of five years. At Southern Cross we changed into the Government train, and I travelled through the night in a compartment with four others, two of whom were ill, one of them suffering from some form of ophthalmia which caused him excruciating pain and kept him the whole time awake. None of us obtained much sleep, and we were glad to reach Perth early next morning.

Thus ended my trip to the goldfields, upon which I look back with considerable satisfaction in spite of the obvious discomforts which it entailed. I found that all with whom I came in contact in Western Australia, and, I might add, in Australasia, whether they were custom-house officials, railway employés, hotel proprietors or servants, had done their best to be obliging. Of the kindly hospitality of all whom I met on the goldfields I cannot speak in sufficiently high terms. They were uniformly straightforward, generous, energetic men, who gave me the impression of a good moral standard. I do not speak of the adventurers who congregate in any place where money can be made rapidly by unscrupulous methods, but of the managers, foremen and others, who are directly engaged in the development of the mines. The great curse of the mining districts, and also, to some extent, of Perth, is the absence of sufficient means of recreation. This state of things may be inevitable in the case of towns of very recent growth, but its result is, that men who have worked all day, requiring some form of diversion, find it in drink. But, in spite of the large consumption of liquor, drunkenness is rare and rowdiness almost unknown. At Coolgardie on a Saturday evening the streets were perfectly quiet ; beyond some discordant strains of music, scarcely a sound was to be heard. In spite of one or two recent burglaries, life and property are scarcely less safe than in England. A bank manager who travelled with me from Kalgoorlie told me that, in starting a new branch of his bank at an outlying township, he had been obliged at first to live in, and keep his money in, a tent, but that on no occasion had he been menaced by the slightest attempt at robbery. I shall long remember the sight of townships which have sprung up where a few years ago was nothing but bush, and promise to become the scene of great industrial activity, and my intercourse with some of the pioneers of the mining movement, men who have penetrated hundreds of miles into the interior of the country, have endured for years the terrible hardships of life in the bush, and have, by their untiring exertions, seconded by the influx of capital following upon their success, done much to raise Western Australia to a prominent position among the Provinces of the Southern Hemisphere.

INDEX

———•◇•———

317

The Gresham Press,

UNWIN BROTHERS,

WOKING AND LONDON.

A FIRST FLEET FAMILY: BEING A HITHERTO UNPUBLISHED NARRATIVE OF CERTAIN REMARKABLE ADVENTURES COMPILED FROM THE PAPERS OF SERGEANT WILLIAM DEW, OF THE MARINES

BY

LOUIS BECKE and WALTER JEFFERY

Second Edition. Crown 8vo., cloth, **6s.**

"As convincingly real and vivid as a narrative can be."—*Sketch.*

"No maker of plots could work out a better story of its kind, nor balance it more neatly."—*Daily Chronicle.*

"A book which describes a set of characters varied and so attractive as the more prominent figures in this romance, and a book so full of life, vicissitude, and peril, should be welcomed by every discreet novel reader."—*Yorkshire Post.*

"A very interesting tale, written in clear and vigorous English."—*Globe.*

"The novel is a happy blend of truth and fiction, with a purpose that will be appreciated by many readers; it has also the most exciting elements of the tale of adventure."
Morning Post.

11, Paternoster Buildings, London, E.C.

WORKS BY JOSEPH CONRAD

I.

AN OUTCAST OF THE ISLANDS

Crown 8vo., cloth, **6s.**

"Subject to the qualifications thus disposed of (*vide* first part of notice), 'An Outcast of the Islands' is perhaps the finest piece of fiction that has been published this year, as 'Almayer's Folly' was one of the finest that was published in 1895 . . . Surely this is real romance—the romance that is real. Space forbids anything but the merest recapitulation of the other living realities of Mr. Conrad's invention—of Lingard, of the inimitable Almayer, the one-eyed Babalatchi, the Naturalist, of the pious Abdulla—all novel, all authentic. Enough has been written to show Mr. Conrad's quality. He imagines his scenes and their sequence like a master ; he knows his individualities and their hearts ; he has a new and wonderful field in this East Indian Novel of his. . . . Greatness is deliberately written ; the present writer has read and re-read his two books, and after putting this review aside for some days to consider the discretion of it, the word still stands."—*Saturday Review*

II.

ALMAYER'S FOLLY

Second Edition. Crown 8vo., cloth, **6s.**

"This startling, unique, splendid book."

Mr. T. P. O'CONNOR, M.P.

"This is a decidedly powerful story of an uncommon type, and breaks fresh ground in fiction. . . . All the leading characters in the book—Almayer, his wife, his daughter, and Dain, the daughter's native lover—are well drawn, and the parting between father and daughter has a pathetic naturalness about it, unspoiled by straining after effect. There are, too, some admirably graphic passages in the book. The approach of a monsoon is most effectively described. . . . The name of Mr. Joseph Conrad is new to us, but it appears to us as if he might become the Kipling of the Malay Archipelago."—*Spectator.*

T. FISHER UNWIN, Publisher,

THE EBBING OF THE TIDE

BY

LOUIS BECKE

Author of " By Reef and Palm "

Second Edition. Crown 8vo., cloth, **6s.**

❦

" Mr. Louis Becke wields a powerful pen, with the additional advantage that he waves it in unfrequented places, and summons up with it the elemental passions of human nature. . . . It will be seen that Mr. Becke is somewhat of the fleshly school, but with a pathos and power not given to the ordinary professors of that school. . . Altogether for those who like stirring stories cast in strange scenes, this is a book to be read."—*National Observer.*

PACIFIC TALES

BY

LOUIS BECKE

With a Portrait of the Author

Second Edition. Crown 8vo., cloth, **6s.**

❦

" The appearance of a new book by Mr. Becke has become an event of note —and very justly. No living author, if we except Mr. Kipling, has so amazing a command of that unhackneyed vitality of phrase that most people call by the name of realism. Whether it is scenery or character or incident that he wishes to depict, the touch is ever so dramatic and vivid that the reader is conscious of a picture and impression that has no parallel save in the records of actual sight and memory."— *Westminster Gazette.*

"Another series of sketches of island life in the South Seas, not inferior to those contained in ' By Reef and Palm.' "—*Speaker.*

"The book is well worth reading. The author knows what he is talking about and has a keen eye for the picturesque."—G. B. BURGIN in *To-day.*

" A notable contribution to the romance of the South Seas."
T. P. O'CONNOR, M.P., in *The Graphic.*

11, Paternoster Buildings, London, E.C.

T. FISHER UNWIN, Publisher,

PADDY'S WOMAN

BY

HUMPHREY JAMES

Crown 8vo., **6s.**

" Traits of the Celt of humble circumstances are copied with keen appreciation and unsparing accuracy." *Scotsman*.

". . . . . . . They are full of indescribable charm and pathos."—*Bradford Observer*.

" The outstanding merit of this series of stories is that they are absolutely true to life . . . . the photographic accuracy and minuteness displayed are really marvellous."
Aberdeen Free Press.

" ' Paddy's Woman and Other Stories ' by Humphrey James ; a volume written in the familiar diction of the Ulster people themselves, with **perfect realism and very remarkable ability. . . . For genuine human nature and human relations, and humour of an indescribable kind, we are unable to cite a rival to this volume.**"
The World.

" For a fine subtle piece of humour we are inclined to think that ' **A Glass of Whisky** ' takes a lot of beating . . In short Mr. Humphrey James has given us a delightful book, and one which does as much credit to his heart as to his head. We shall look forward with a keen anticipation to the next ' writings ' by this shrewd, ' cliver,' and compassionate young author."—*Bookselling*.

11, Paternoster Buildings, London, E.C.

www.ingramcontent.com/pod-product-compliance
Lightning Source LLC
Chambersburg PA
CBHW021113270326
41929CB00009B/864